Who Am I Without Him?

May you find your husband who loves you most in the pages of this book & may changed you be forever changed & blessed as you meet Him here.

Gail Ruth Peterson

10-8-12

GAIL RUTH PETERSON

Who Am I Without Him?

TATE PUBLISHING
AND ENTERPRISES, LLC

This book is designed to provide accurate and authoritative information with regard to the subject matter covered. This information is given with the understanding that neither the author nor Tate Publishing, LLC is engaged in rendering legal, professional advice. Since the details of your situation are fact dependent, you should additionally seek the services of a competent professional.

The opinions expressed by the author are not necessarily those of Tate Publishing, LLC.

Published by Tate Publishing & Enterprises, LLC
127 E. Trade Center Terrace | Mustang, Oklahoma 73064 USA
1.888.361.9473 | www.tatepublishing.com

Tate Publishing is committed to excellence in the publishing industry. The company reflects the philosophy established by the founders, based on Psalm 68:11,
"The Lord gave the word and great was the company of those who published it."

Book design copyright © 2012 by Tate Publishing, LLC. All rights reserved.
Cover design by Lauro Talibong
Interior design by Nathan Harmony

Published in the United States of America

ISBN: 978-1-62147-476-0
1. Religion / Christian Life / Death, Grief, Bereavement
2. Self-Help / Death, Grief, Bereavement
12.09.25

Dedication

This book is dedicated to my daughters and late husband, Vinnie.

To my girls: Love for one another has glued our family together over the years through adventures and joy as well as indescribable fear, brokenness and pain. Love for one another has also allowed us to become the women God created us to be. I could not have written this book or moved on with my life if you did not eventually find it in your hearts to accept, honor, respect and love the new woman God would emerge from beneath the layers of this aging skin. I know it's been so hard to lose your Daddy, but in some ways you lost your Mommy too as I've been molded and reshaped by our Heavenly Husband. I trust you will always remember that God knows what He's doing. Keep being conduits of God's spirit that lives inside you and not just containers, as we only discover who we were really meant to be when we not only let God fill us with with love but also experience it as a part of us when we pour it out on others.

To Vinnie: Losing the man who loved me for twenty-five years of marriage, and his ceaseless desire to work hard to provide for his family and me over the years, created the aching hole in my heart when he died, a hole that put me in a desperate search for a new depth of relationship with God to soothe the pain of my loss. It was a desperation that eventually compelled me to write. It is the depth of his love while he lived that made it so heartbreaking when he died. It is the extent of his protection and provision in our marriage that made it natural to try finding it in his absence in my heavenly husband, who knew every tiny ache in my heart.

Finding answers and a new depth of intimacy with God led me to journal and eventually compile my writings into this book that might help others in their desperate search for God's path for their life. Thank you for loving me so well, Vinnie. As your family said for weeks before you departed this planet, "We'll see you later!"

Acknowledgments

To my dear friend Jodi, who took me under her wing when Vinnie died, trained me to work with others in grief ministry, and encouraged me to seek God's purpose for my life after his death. She has continued to remind me that God has a plan for my life to serve Him and others in grief ministry and most specifically to widows. Thank you, my friend, for seeing God-given potential in me to help others in grief and widowhood. It's been an honor to serve with you these past four years. Without your encouragement to seek the Lord and to write about my journey, I may still be lost in sorrow without direction or purpose.

To my new and dear husband, Mike, who not only fell in love with my extreme personality but also my desire to live for a God-filled purpose. He has been encouraging me to write since he first read my work, reminding me often to use the gifts God's given me to communicate with others in words on paper. You'll never know how much your encouragement means to me; without it, this book would have died when discouragement peeked its ugly head in along the way.

To my home church that rose to the mandate of caring for the first widow in our church family, not because you had to but because you love the Lord so well. Your kindness to me in my widowhood can never be expressed in words of this world. And without answering the urgent call to teach the truth in Scripture with conviction and without apology, I would probably have grown a mushy faith that would have rocked me off the planet when Vinnie died. Thank you especially to my pastor, Larry, for making yourself available to me when I needed advice, for your patience with me when I was about to make choices based on confusion, for bringing clarity to my thinking during those times, for the integrity in the teaching of the Word, and for excellent discipleship. This book is the product of your teaching.

Table of Contents

Part One:

Introduction

Introduction

My husband died in August 2008 after a ten-month battle with bladder cancer. As prepared as I thought I was for his departure home to be with our Lord, I found myself struggling when he died, as many who have lost a loved one do.

Until that time, I'd only lost one person close to me. It was an uncle who was like a father to me when I was growing up. But when he died, I'd already been living hundreds of miles away for several years. Though his death was sad and rattled my heart, my life had already adjusted to living life without him. That grief journey was not very long.

The year my husband died, we had already lost twin grandbabies, and my stepson died two months after my husband's death. I also lost an aunt, an uncle, and four friends that year, with one to murder. The pain of sorrow was almost unbearable at times. I struggled to figure out what life was to look like for me now that the Lord had me living life all by myself (the children were all married that year and left me an official empty nester). The absence of my loved ones left many holes in my heart and in my world. Life as I knew it had ended.

I am a woman whose strongest spiritual gift is faith. My relationship with the Lord had been a very intimate one for many years. That part of my journey in grief never changed; I never doubted He was with me during one of the darkest, lowest times in my life. But I did wrestle with God during many of the early days in my grief journey, trying to figure out what He had in store for me and my life after so much loss and sorrow. I tried to understand who I was and was to become now that the role of wife, "the other half," and many of my coupled friendships began slipping away.

The lack of ability to focus and concentrate in the first year of Vinnie's death (I later learned this is a very common symptom of grief) had me failing in my work as an administrative assistant, in spite of almost thirty years in this type work. I wondered what was to become of my work. Even my role as "mommy" was rapidly changing, with all the children married, three of which were married only months before Vinnie passed. It was clear that I had found my confidence and security in these roles over the years, even though I often didn't feel I filled the roles very well. I knew deep down in my heart that ultimately I was a child of God and a bride to Jesus, but the adjustment, coupled with grief, was overwhelming to discern.

During this time of wrestling, an out-of-state friend sent me an encouraging e-mail that truly began to shape my grief journey and aided in the steps to true healing.

She lost her father the year before Vinnie died. She sent me the same verse that she hoped her mother would be encouraged by just one year before, hoping it would also encourage me. She may never know how much that e-mail and that verse impacted my life that day!

> For your Maker is your husband—the LORD Almighty is his name—the Holy One of Israel is your Redeemer; he is called the God of all the earth.
>
> Isaiah 54:5 (NIV)

Though I'd read this passage before, that day it was as if I read it for the first time. It took on new meaning that day. It brought up challenges and even questions I began to ask God. Little did I know that day that I'd keep asking questions about its meaning and that the questions and seeming answers would develop into this book!

The passage is packed with implications of who God is, who I am, and what kind of relationship He longs to have with me and longs to have with all who are His bride, the members of His Church. I struggled to grasp it all. I read it religiously every day for months. As the many questions came to mind and

I began to journal the questions and what I sensed might be some of God's answers. I continued to pray that God would help me understand this powerfully significant verse in a real and applicable way.

I wanted to understand how God could make such a claim to *be* my (our) husband. I thought of some of the areas I was missing in my relationship with Vinnie, and I began to wonder how on earth God could claim to be my husband when I knew He would not come down and fulfill all the roles that Vinnie filled in my life. Yet I was mesmerized by the fact that the verse does not say that God is *like* my husband; it says He *is* my husband!

It was perplexing. I daresay that eventually I began to challenge God with my thoughts. *Lord, I cannot snuggle up with you at night and wrap my cold feet around your warm legs. I cannot ask you to pick up something at the store on the way home from work because I am running late. You will not be mowing my lawn or fixing any leaks in a pipe or ceiling. How can you fill these roles of my husband? How can you claim to be my husband? Do you have a means, a way, a plan to fill these empty areas of my life now? You know the areas I'm missing, and you know Vinnie's gone, so how will you fulfill this role for me?*

I was missing more than just the man himself. I was missing the man who took me on dates and the man I shared my inner thoughts and ideas with. I wanted to know if or how God would replace Vinnie in all of these areas.

I also wanted to understand the significance of God as my Maker and husband at the same time, as it's stated in this verse. For several months I wrote down the many questions that this verse brought to mind and the answers that seemed to become clear in my meditation and prayer. Over time I was beginning to understand and know God like I never did before. I was beginning to see a love He had for me that ran deeper than skin or circumstance, and I knew that I was just beginning to dig through a treasure that God had in store for me. I also became increasingly confident that God absolutely loved that I was willing to wrestle with Him over all this. What seemed at first to be a lack of faith in Him proved to be a true testimony of faith. I realized that one can't wrestle with an unreality! I had not questioned God telling me He *is* my husband but rather I struggled to understand *how* He is my husband—all the time affirming His existence.

The more I dug into the treasure and meaning of His promises and proclamations in this verse, my love for Him grew deeper. The deeper my love grew, the more burdened I became to help others see how much our Maker loves each one of His beloved children. I spent time reflecting on His love and even stopped to think of my own past, a childhood of fear, guilt, and depression, and how much God loved me then, but I didn't know it. I thought about my marriage to Vinnie, one that was filled with ups and downs, and trials and blessings, and how many of those blessings came because of my relationship with my Maker. I began to wonder how many people were hurting all around me and had no idea that their Maker desired an intimate relationship with them. I wondered, *How many people does God want to experience a great joy in Him even in the midst of deep sadness and broken, seemingly hopeless circumstances, such as broken marriages, wayward children, or widowhood?*

I began to ask God how I could share with other women what I was beginning to discover about Him in this powerfully packed verse. Thus grew the passion to compile this little book.

Who Are the Children of God and Bride of the Maker?

Before we can examine what a relationship with our Maker might look like, we have to acknowledge that sin is the very thing that has prevented humankind from knowing an intimate relationship with Him. What is a sinner? Is it being a murderer, a thief, or a rapist? Yes, it's fair to say that is sin. But sin is so much more than just being a "bad person!" Sin is being less than what God made us to be. Sin is doing anything other than what God intended us to do. And without Jesus, it is not possible to be or do what we were purposed to. Without doing and being what we were designed for, we can't possibly experience a total satisfaction and fulfillment in our lives, at least over the long haul. If you have known success in some area of your life but still feel emptiness in your heart, may I suggest that something intangible is missing? God has made it clear that the hole I used to have in my heart was a longing to know my Maker like never, ever before!

Sin is our inability to go a whole day without being irritated or inpatient with someone. Sin is like cyanide in a glass of clear water. Even one drop in a glass of water, though small and totally invisible, will poison the drink. One drop of imperfection in us keeps us from truly knowing a holy God. It's impossible for a sinful person to be anywhere near holy ground because we would make the ground unholy. One smidgen of discontent, discord, or imperfection of any size, not to mention a lie, a cheat, or not obeying a simple traffic law, keeps us separated from a holy God.

God knew that humans could never redeem themselves from the inevitable effects of sin. The penalty of sin is death (Romans 6:23). There is only one punishment for sin: death. However, God made mankind to have a sweet, loving relationship with Him. He made us to be His hands and feet on earth, to partner with Him in caring for all that He created. God has been longing for the people He created to have this relationship with Him, a relationship He intended all along but that sin has made impossible. There could be only one solution for us, and God orchestrated that too! We'll never grasp Him as our husband if we don't accept His gift of life to us (Jesus Christ) first.

In order to understand how God made a way for us to move from a place where it's impossible to know God, it is important at this point to understand who Jesus is. When Jesus was alive, He spoke some powerful and very important words that many miss in today's multi-religion world. He said, "I am the Way, and the Truth, and the Life. No one comes to the Father except through me" (John 14:6). There are many that know *of* Jesus, and those who even appreciate His teaching or see Him as a great prophet, but what is often missed is that God Himself came to earth as a real man to take upon Himself the penalty of sin for us. He did this for the simple purpose of making it possible for us to know and experience a personal relationship with our heavenly Father. We must understand that it's the only way we could have an intimate relationship with God the Father, because no human man, except one completely free of sin, could do it. If we miss all this, we miss the whole point of His being here. He was not just a good teacher or prophet. There have already been so many of those. Man can't save man; only God could come and do this for us.

When Jesus, the one and only Son of God, came to earth, it was for the sole purpose of taking the sin of this world upon Himself. All those who believe in Him are forgiven and made clean. He paid our penalty for us; He died the death in our place. Putting our trust in that makes a way for us to know God as our Maker, as our husband, as the God Almighty, and as all the other aspects of Himself that He reveals in Scripture and in this one verse alone!

Without the cross, we are faced with a huge gap between God and us. No matter how much good work we do, jumping the cavity will cause us to fall. To get to God by way of the cross is to believe that there is a cross and that we need it. It is to understand that we can't know who we were made to be without knowing the Maker. If we believe, then there is a cross bridging the gap.

Scriptures offer much more detail about our condition and the plan of God's salvation.

1. First we must recognize and admit to God that we are sinners. Being a sinner simply means that we have lived life outside of God's will and outside His design and His love for us.

   For all have sinned, and come short of the glory of God.

   Romans 3:23

2. Once we admit that we have fallen short of God's purpose and glory, we must turn from sin (repent). *Repent* is a word most people don't like to hear, so allow me to shed some light on the meaning of this word. One translation of the original text refers to repent as "turn away." Turning away is different than saying, "I'm sorry and won't do it again." It's saying, "I'm sorry," and walking so far away from it that one's life begins to change.

   In the past God overlooked such ignorance, but now he commands all people everywhere to repent.

   Acts 17:30

3. A penalty has to be paid for the sin of each person separated from God. No human could ever help us make it to God, to heaven. One God could make this happen, and He did! Believe that Jesus Christ died for you, was buried, and rose from the dead. He died for us (while we were still sinners—no need to get our act together first!) so we might have life, eternal life, with our Maker!

> For God so loved the world that he gave his one and only Son, that whoever believes in him shall not perish but have eternal life.
>
> John 3:16

> But God demonstrates his own love for us in this: While we were still sinners, Christ died for us.
>
> Romans 5:8

4. Confess, repent, and express your trust in the act of Christ on the cross through prayer; invite Jesus into your life to become your personal Savior. Accept His invitation to you to have eternal life!

For "everyone who calls on the name of the Lord will be saved."

Romans 10:13

Yet to all who received him, to those who believed in his name, he gave the right to become children of God.

John 1:12

Therefore, if anyone is in Christ, he is a new creation; the old has gone, the new has come!

2 Corinthians 5:17

If you desire to grow in a love relationship with God and trust your life in Him, pray. Ask God to forgive you and to come be the Lord of your life, to make you a new creature in Christ. You might wish to pray the following prayer:

> Dear heavenly Father, my Maker, my husband, I want to know your love for me. I want to experience you as my husband and my heavenly Father. I know that my life has fallen short of experiencing you and the goodness and purpose you have for my

life. I ask that you forgive all the sin that has ever stood in the gap of knowing you. I understand that Jesus, your only Son, came to earth to take on the penalty of death for my sins. He died and rose again so that I might have a new life in Christ. I pray you forgive me and allow me to become a new creation, one that lives for you and with you and seeks your will for my life. Make me useful and give my life purpose as I seek you in the days that lie ahead. Comfort me as I walk the road before me in this difficult and broken world where sorrow and suffering is inevitable but joy in you is still an option, and reveal to me all the ways that you are my husband, especially when I feel alone. It's in Jesus's name I pray. Amen.

If you have prayed for God's love to lead you into a new life with Jesus Christ, it is recommended that you begin to do some of the things listed below.

1. Read your Bible every day to get to know Christ better. "Your word is a lamp to my feet and a light for my path" (Psalm 119:105).

2. Talk to God in prayer every day. "Do not be anxious about anything, but in everything, by prayer and petition, with thanksgiving, present your requests to God" (Philippians 4:6).

3. Participate in areas of the church and fellowship, such as:

   - Serve with other Christians in the church and community.

   - Regularly attend a good church where Christ is preached and the Bible is the final authority.

   - Be baptized, even if you were baptized as a baby. It is a ceremony, much like a wedding, where we demonstrate to friends and family a representation of a commitment we've made with our God.

Let us not give up meeting together, as some are in the habit of doing, but let us encourage one another—and all the more as you see the Day approaching.

Hebrews 10:25

4. Tell others about Christ. "He said to them, 'Go into all the world and preach the good news to all creation'" (Mark 16:15).

If you have accepted Christ as your Lord and Savior, practicing these steps and disciplines will strengthen your relationship with God your Husband.

No one can replace the unique roles, characteristics, and personality of one's husband, and no one is meant to. No one can fulfill the deepest yearnings we might long for in our husband (present one if married or one hoped for). Even the best husband in the world will fall short of satisfying us in every way. But God's mercy and grace is vastly bigger than our wildest imagination. He placed your spouse and other people and circumstances in your life, and He desires you to seek Him to fill all your needs, physically, emotionally, and mentally, in Him, especially when the loved ones around us don't fulfill those needs. He knows that whether you are married or not, emptiness haunts the heart of the widow, a difficult marriage, or the heart of one who remains undesirably single. Most of us live with huge holes in our hearts.

The good news is that He has a plan for each of us, not just a role to play and a job to do, but He also wants us to know who we were meant to be, who He created us to be. He has a plan to help us discover who we were made to be, and God is ready to fill that hole with Himself. He wants to take you and me on a journey, a new journey that can start right now to a deeper place with Him. He longs to take us to a deep and secret chamber few people discover in this lifetime; there are few because most are busy chasing other things to fill the empty places in their hearts. It's not His desire that we choose things that appear to be a quick fix—faster, clearer, more substantial (supposed) means of joy and fulfillment. He longs to take us to a place where we experience a deep, intimate relationship with Him in the person of Jesus. He loves His women. He wants you to know this deeply and to be like the new bride—totally in love with Him too!

As I unpack my story and the passage, I hope you will be as encouraged as I have been by God's love and amazing promises. I hope you will soak in the depth found in Isaiah 54:5 and allow it to minister to you for days and weeks and even months. It's a powerful, life-changing, thought-altering message and a reminder of just how intricate God is and how He so longs to have an amazing relationship with His women.

Getting the Greatest Use of this Book

The remainder of this book is written in two major sections. The first half of the book is the story (from my journal) starting from the time we discovered Vinnie's cancer, the ten months we battled the cancer, his death, and my early struggles as a widow. It's important to understand the walk of faith that happened in my mind and heart before understanding the challenge I put on myself and God; these are challenges I hope you'll be called to take on by the time you move onto the second section of these pages. The questions mixed throughout the second half of the book challenge our walk, view, and relationship with God and help us understand God more and cling more tightly to the promises He's left for us to trust when life is sorrowful and hard.

While these tough questions and elements of new understanding are vital for the potential transformation to happen in our relationship with God, it's also important to know the struggle that I faced before I hammered out tough questions to God as presented in my story, which, by the way, I proclaim to be God's story. Even the title of this book is completely accredited to the Lord's anointing; it's His story!

The second half of the book is meditative and reflective, centered in this passage in Isaiah. As you move from one section to the next in the second half of the book, feel free to go back and forth throughout the sections as the Lord brings things to your mind. This study does not have to be completed in a few days or a particular number of weeks. There is no time frame in which it should be finished. You may visit some sections repeatedly, and other sections may only be visited once. You may also want to come back and visit the thoughts and answers that you journal in all the sections many months or even years from now, just to examine the progress you've made in drawing closer to God. That could bring great excitement and encouragement.

It is recommended that you move through the back half of the book initially in chronological order. If you find yourself camping out in one section for a while, that's fine. If you feel led to go back to a previous section, that's also fine, but when you move on, pick up at the last place you left and continue forward.

Remember that healing, restoration, and transformation is a long process—long but not impossible to see to the other end. Time alone doesn't heal one's pain, but time is an important element of the process. The best method of healing is time mixed with intention. There are just some things that won't go away by themselves, no matter how much time passes. Every single thought must become captive and examined in the light of Scripture. This one passage from Isaiah alone will shed plenty of light for us to begin a deeper walk with the Lord and create long, strong, deep roots in being confident in who we are in Christ and the joy found in both.

This study is for you to savor. It doesn't matter if it takes a month or a year, or even a few years until you feel you have gone through it all. Relax. It's all in God's timetable, and He will use every aspect of it to bring you close to Him and make you see how beautiful you truly are to Him. It might feel like you're struggling to discern who you are now without him (husband), but it's my prayer that you'll be confident in who you are *with* Him or in Him when you can say you have completed your work in this book.

Part Two:

The Journey

The Journey Started

How many times have I heard people say, "It seems like only yesterday"? I hate that phrase, and yet in my case, it is true. I remember so many details of the day it's scary. It was October 21, 2007. I was on my way to church, and it was rather early for a Saturday morning. We were hosting a Women's Day event at the church, and I was teaching a session. I left the house around 7:30 a.m. to get my classroom ready. On the way there, I turned on the car radio, which I rarely do. I don't like radio noise first thing in the morning.

The radio is always tuned to K-Love radio (unless one of my daughters borrows the car and changes the channel). A woman was talking about how she had survived cancer and had prayed that God would somehow provide her financially with a circumstance that would enable her to minister and encourage other cancer patients. Her prayer was answered in an amazing way; her oncologist called her and offered her a full-time job to visit his patients to pray with them!

As I listened to this story, it dawned on me that I had not really known anyone close to me with cancer. I worked with two different women who had breast cancer, but their cases were each caught early, and they survived after chemotherapy. Besides, they were associates at work, and I also wasn't very close to them, if you know what I mean. I felt compelled to pray that God would prepare my heart to one day hear the heartbreaking news that someone I deeply loved would be diagnosed with cancer. After all, I was getting older, and odds were I'd know someone soon who would have it. Deep down in the quiet place of my heart, I thought I might one day hear this dreadful news in regard to my mother.

After Women's Day, Vinnie arrived to help a crew of other men move chairs and get the worship center back in place for the Sunday morning services. He stopped me before he entered the building and casually mentioned that his urologist called him earlier that day. He'd been referred to a urologist when a seemingly stubborn bladder infection would not go away. It had been causing Vinnie discomfort off and on for almost a year! The doctor called him while I was doing my workshop, just a few hours after praying in the car for God to prepare my heart. The doctor reported the test results: he had a tumor in the bladder. Vinnie had cancer.

As horrible as the news was, I was also overwhelmed by the fact that God, my heavenly Father, was so gracious and kind that He (the Holy Spirit) prompted me to turn that radio on earlier that morning and compelled me to pray for my heart to be prepared. God was doing just that the whole time. What a loving God! Perhaps there are some people who would have been mad at God for allowing their spouse and friend of almost twenty-five years to get cancer in the first place, but I never saw it that way. I knew people got cancer. It's one of the results of living in a fallen world, a world far removed from the utopia we were meant to live in, the beautiful garden that God originally made for us. And if Christians can't be light in the struggle of cancer, how will anyone else see God when they need to most, when they may be close to the end of their time on earth?

No, I wasn't upset that God "let this happen," as some might see it. Cancer happens. I will never forget how very blessed I felt that afternoon that out of abundant compassion, my God prepared me to hear this terribly sad news.

Though Vinnie, who was convinced by the doctors, insisted that this type of surgery was easy to treat if caught early, I knew deep down in my heart that we were in for a very long journey. I do believe that Vinnie knew, as somewhere deep in my own heart I knew, that he would die from the cancer. I didn't know when. I didn't want to believe it, and I was given hope several times from doctors and thought (and hoped) many times that I was wrong, that he would survive it. He didn't.

I am terribly sad that Vinnie is no longer here with me. I miss his crazy voice and that Italian accent of his! I long to hear it sometimes, and though it makes me cry like a baby, I like to listen to his voice that I have on a CD.

My pain, sorrow, and sadness are still quite raw, and I am still trying to figure out what life without Vinnie is supposed to be like. I guess I will have a different lifestyle now. It is hard to accept the title of widow, but that is what I am now—a widow. It will be a long road to travel, an adventure I don't really want, but I am still here, and I don't want to live without joy. So I look for ways to experience joy with family and friends. I have an awesome Shepherd who will be holding my hand as I walk this road and some pretty awesome people in my life too.

A Very Bumpy Ride

Vinnie had his first surgery in early November. I went to the hospital with him early in the morning. Besides giving birth to our girls, neither of us ever had a hospital stay since we had known each other. The kids were all planning to come later in the day, but none of us were concerned. After all, the doctors insisted this was not going to be a big deal and the cancer would be easy to treat. Vinnie seemed unclear about whether the tumor found in the bladder was cancerous, or at least that is what he said, but I'm not sure if he was really confused, didn't want to ask questions, or simply didn't want me to worry.

After registering at the hospital, Vinnie and I sat quietly in the waiting room, reading magazines. Perhaps our unusual silence was a product of some anxiety, but we were trying to appear strong and hopeful for one another. While waiting to be called into pre-op, Vinnie suddenly broke silence to read a joke to me that he found in a magazine.

"A college student has an exam coming up and tells the professor that he has a funeral to attend, so he can't make it to the exam. The professor excuses him. When the next exam comes up, the student tells the professor he has another funeral to attend, so the professor excuses him again. Another exam comes up, and the student again tells the professor that he has another funeral so he can't make it. The professor asks, "How many other people in your family are going to die?" The student replies, "Oh, they're not my family. I'm the grave digger."

I didn't think the joke was that funny. I thought it was cute maybe, but it was not that funny to me. Vinnie looked a bit disappointed (perhaps his attempt to wipe away any fears I might be hiding by making me smile) but still chuckling at the humor he saw in this quirky joke, he turned away and said he would tell the kids; they'd think it was funny. That was about the most of our conversation that morning. Perhaps we just didn't want to acknowledge a silent concern brewing deep inside each of our hearts.

Suddenly he got called in to pre-op, and all the kids arrived just in time for them to see him before he was taken up to the operating room, a procedure that was supposed to be outpatient surgery. We gave him kisses and waited together in the waiting room.

The procedure was only supposed to last an hour. I began to wonder if something was wrong when it took almost two hours before the doctor came out to talk to us. When we finally saw his urologist, his look of deep concern was hard for him to hide. He began by telling me that it was very invasive and that he wasn't sure he "got all of it." He said he'd have to wait to hear what the pathologist report would conclude. He just didn't seem sure that the surgery had helped Vinnie. Not having been completely convinced that Vinnie had cancer prior to this surgery, I looked at the doctor at one point and asked, "Does my husband have cancer?"

That poor doctor was so sorry to have to tell me, "Yes. I thought you knew." I suppose deep down I did know, but I just had to hear it directly from the doctor himself.

Ironically, when Vinnie and I were about to be married, he suggested that I prepare myself to be a young widow. He could not explain why, but he had just always had a sensing that he would die young. I never forgot those words. At one point earlier in our marriage when the physicians were concerned about his liver (he had hepatitis B at some point in his life), I thought maybe he'd die like his father did. His dad's liver failed to function, and he went into a coma and died almost a month later. His dad died at age sixty-two. But eventually Vinnie pulled through that period of low liver function. That was when I had hope that maybe he wasn't really going to die young and that we'd grow old together and travel alone in our RV, visiting America. We never owned an RV, but it was our dream.

Here I was twenty-four years into our marriage and was now being told that my husband had cancer—for sure—and that the doctor wasn't sure they got it all. Was this it? Would cancer be the cause of an early death? The doctors continued to give me hope that he was still young, strong, and would easily make it through this. I was given hope that he'd make it even when they told me the next day that they didn't get all the cancer and the bladder would have to be removed. My heart sank, but I wanted the fear in my heart to be wrong. I wanted to know that he was going to be okay. I wanted to know that we were not going to go down a long, hard road of him being a very sick man. I wanted to believe that we'd get that RV and travel one day. I wanted to believe that after all the hard years of marriage, we'd have sweet time ahead of us. I wanted to believe it. The doctors seemed to believe it, but I knew deep down in my heart that it was a real possibility that he wasn't going to make it. I kept hoping anyway. I kept praying for him to be healed and well again.

Vinnie purchased a lime-green minibike just a few months before he was sick. He rode the grandchildren around on it up and down our long dirt driveway and drove it to work when the weather permitted. He was so proud to be saving so much gas money on his new wheels! I wanted to hear that crazy green bike come chugging down the driveway once more. I wanted to look at the window once more with concern that he might tip that bike over. I'd rather him hurt from a bike fall than to suffer with cancer. He never rode that bike again after his surgery. But for many, many months, we were to travel on a very bumpy road.

It Really Wasn't Funny!

Vinnie was such a joker; he loved to make people laugh. When we were at someone's home, a party, or some kind of social event, Vinnie was the life of the party. He always had a joke to tell—or several jokes, especially Catholic jokes, which was especially funny because of his Catholic upbringing and his Italian accent. Our family will forever remember his favorite.

While traveling to Italy, Michael Jordan runs into a friend at the airport who is going to the Vatican to see the Pope, and he invites Michael to come along with him. When they get there, they are escorted into the gardens to wait for the Pope to come out. They end up waiting a long time. Michael, being the tall man that he is, gets hungry while waiting and he reaches up to grab some apples from a tree in the garden. He eats them and throws the cores on the ground. The two men wait a while longer, and Michael gets hungry again. He grabs more apples, eats them, and throws the cores on the ground. When this happens again, the Pope finally comes out to meet them. He goes directly to Michael, waves his hands up, down, and side to side, as if he is blessing him, and immediately goes back inside. Michael's friend (who originally went to the Vatican to be blessed by the Pope) goes to Michael and says, "Hey, man, what was that about? I came here to be blessed by the Pope, but instead he blessed you and walked away without a word to me!" Surprised by his friend's reaction, Michael replies, "What are you talking about? He didn't bless me. He said (while motioning hands), 'Stop taking my apples from the tree and throwing them on the ground. Now get out of here!'"

He had a closet full of riddles too that he'd pull out to keep kids busy (and grownup kids too). In a room with children and access to paper and pens, he would ask them to figure how the man put his ten horses in nine stalls. He'd add that no walls could be expanded and that no stall had more than one horse. He'd wait patiently while kids (and adults) would ask all sorts of questions, scribbling diagrams of horses and stalls. Vinnie would continue smirking as he watched piles of eraser dust blow off tabletops and inquisitive minds unable to capture the simplicity of his riddle. When all attempts were exhausted, he'd drawn nine stalls and write these letters, one letter per stall: T-E-N-H-O-R-S-E-S (that's nine letters in the nine stalls). He'd give himself a funny little invisible pat on the back for cleverness and go right onto the next joke stored away in his box of fun.

After Vinnie's first surgery where the tumor was removed from the bladder, he was wheeled up to the fifth floor and kept overnight. All the kids had arrived by the end of the day, and we all waited in his room for him to wake up. We waited almost an hour for him to come out of anesthesia. I'd never seen Vinnie so quiet. He almost looked dead, and I remember wondering if he'd look like that when he'd die, but that day wouldn't be the day. That day he'd wake up and be okay.

It seemed a long time before he began to show signs of coming around from after the surgery. The room was tiny, a bit claustrophobic for a good-size man in a bed with four grown children and a wife standing over him almost breathlessly waiting for him to wake up. Then it happened. He suddenly opened one eye. He rolled that one eye around for a minute as if his brain were a video camera carefully taking a picture in his mind of each one of us in the room. After assessing his company, he slowly opened the other eye and again glanced a moment to take inventory of each person watching over him.

His eyes now wide open but his expression still set in stone, like he had while under anesthesia, he said nothing for several minutes, and then he suddenly opened his mouth. Out popped that crazy joke he read to me early in the morning from the magazine! Even with a straight face, he rattled that joke off his lips like he'd been telling it for years. I couldn't believe it! What did he do, go over that joke a hundred times in his mind all through surgery so he wouldn't forget it?

While the kids all laughed, relieved that their daddy was acting normal, I stood there in disbelief. I was happy to see the family behaving their usual loud selves, but it was all surreal to me. I knew Vinnie too well. He didn't want any of us to worry. Telling that silly joke, bringing laughter into the room, was his way of giving hope to the family that everything was going to be okay now and we shouldn't worry. It was a tight squeeze for all five of us in that tiny room, but I felt distant, watching it all somehow from a distance, an invisible distance, wondering if everything was okay as Vinnie was trying to portray or was he secretly wondering, as I was, if this battle was really over. Was he prepared to make this sober bunch of family members quickly get over their fears by telling that dumb joke? It made us all laugh.

I still didn't think the joke was that funny, but I thought Vinnie was. There never will be another guy like Vinnie.

The next morning the doctor came to see Vinnie with results of the pathologist report. There were no kids present; just Vinnie and me. The jokes weren't bubbling out of Vinnie's mouth that morning. The report indicated that he had cancer, and the doctor hadn't removed it all. Vinnie would have to have surgery again, and his bladder would have to be removed. The doctor spent some time with us both, explaining all that would entail and what Vinnie's options were for this procedure. We had no idea that people could have bladders rebuilt inside, and no one would ever know that the bladder was gone. We had hope that the bladder would come out and that he would be able to eat, drink, sleep, swim, and do all the normal things he'd always done, even without a bladder. We were relieved, at least through that upcoming holiday season.

Recovering from the first "simple" procedure of removing the tumor was a taste of what was to come for us. Vinnie began to experience more pain than he ever had before the surgery. At first this seemed normal because, after all, he was recovering from surgery. But over the next few weeks while we waited for an appointment to meet with the surgeons who specialized in the reconstruction of bladders at Duke University, his pain seemed to grow from painful discomfort to agonizing pain.

By the time we finally got to the doctor's office to meet the specialist that would perform the next surgery, Vinnie was in such terrible pain that it was difficult to sit, walk, sleep, stand, or function with any comfort. We were now being told that because the cancer was so invasive, he would have only a 50/50 chance to survive the cancer, with or without any of the choices of reconstructive surgery he would decide on. That was scary news to me. This doctor was a straight shooter. She told it like it was, not like we would hope it would be. She wanted us to know the facts. We appreciated her well-stated facts, but we were also stunned, to put it mildly.

Not only were we stunned about his prognosis, but we were also disappointed to know that he would not even be able to have the surgery until January 31. We would have to wait almost two months for this surgery. The doctor suggested that since we'd have to wait so long for the surgery, it would be best to have chemotherapy first for six months and then do the surgery. Vinnie was in too much pain to wait six months, and he opted to wait only two months for the surgery and have chemotherapy later. We had no idea that the cancer would grow so fast.

He was in agonizing pain day and night. He was always uncomfortable. None of the pain medication seemed to make a dent in the pain levels. He was not himself. Vinnie was deteriorating before me; I just didn't know it. He was beginning to change, slowly, into someone I never knew before. Vinnie and our life together was changing, and it was becoming less and less funny.

A Twist of Events

Waiting for Vinnie's surgery was awful. The holidays were a struggle. He was unbearably uncomfortable. He wasn't his usual funny self; his patience was a tad bit shorter, and he was exhausted. But eventually, January 31 came. We drove to Duke and signed Vinnie in for surgery. The waiting room was only supposed to have two visitors in it. It was crowded, and there were four of us there: my two daughters, one of my future sons-in-law, and me. We hoped the nurses would not ask some of us to leave. I had a bad feeling about this day, but I didn't want the kids to know. I appeared hopeful, expectant, and positive.

Oddly enough, however, about an hour into the expected six-hour surgery, we each began to confess that we had a bad feeling about the surgery. We could not say why or what we thought was going to happen, but we sensed it was not going to be as smooth as we were told it could go. Ten minutes after discussing our bad feelings about the day's outcome, we were invited into a consultation room to get an update on how the surgery was going. I heard other surgeons come talk to the visitors waiting. They reported good results right out in the waiting room. It became obvious why our consultation was in a private room. It was not a good report.

The cancer had grown quite aggressively. During the two-month wait, the cancer had destroyed too much of the ureter (the tube that runs from the kidney to the bladder) to save what was still a perfectly good kidney. Without a ureter, a kidney would have no way of draining. The kidney was good, but it would have to be removed. Vinnie would not get the reconstructive bladder he'd hoped for; he had his left kidney, his bladder, prostate, and lymph nodes removed that day. The many hours we spent weighing the best pros and cons of the different types of surgeries he could have had all seemed pointless. The surgery took ten hours.

Requests for prayer went out days before the surgery to most of our church family and the church members of each of our coworkers. But this sudden new twist in events had urgent prayer requests sent out immediately like fireworks. Several pastors and church leaders came to see us that afternoon. The funny thing is that in spite of us having almost eight visitors at one point, not one hospital staff person said anything about the number of visitors we had the rest of that day. They knew Vinnie was not doing well, that we were in shock, and that we were well loved by many who were concerned. They even gave us access to the phone in the waiting room in pre-op until the call came telling us that he was finally sent to ICU. We were finally able to see Vinnie about twelve hours later. It was an exhausting day.

He seemed barely alive. Dozens of tubes were connected to every region of his frail, weak, pale body. He didn't respond for days. It was scary. It was sad. Once again I began to wonder if this was what it would be like when Vinnie died, but it was not to happen that day.

Three days later, he was finally functionally well enough to leave the ICU and brought up to a room. We began the cumbersome task of learning to change the urostomy bag. There is an art to this task—an art that took weeks to learn. It had to fit exactly right; the skin has to be completely dry (in an area that is not prone to be dry). I had to learn to shave the skin without soap, lotion, or other products that could infect the stoma (the end of the ureter connected to the good kidney that is exposed to the outside of the belly area). It was important to get a good seal unless I wanted to change sheets and wash laundry all day long. Right after surgery the stoma is at its largest, so it takes even longer to learn how to do it because the size and shape change so much until it heals. It was a frustrating task. One day, about a week after he was sent home, I could not get it right. I went through all the remaining six sample bags with the results the same every single time: urine everywhere!

Discouraged and frustrated, I finally took Vinnie to the hospital to see the ostomy nurse to show me, once again, how to adhere the bag without leaking. He sat in the car with a roll of paper towel on his belly! What a fiasco that day was, but eventually I'd learn to do it with perfection.

Even though we were told he'd be in the hospital for ten days, Vinnie was sent home just six days after the kidney had been removed. He hadn't been home more than two days when we noticed that fluid was dribbling down his belly from along the incision. When I took him to the ER, they realized that the stitches in the under layers of his skin had come apart. He was immediately accepted from the emergency room and led upstairs for a sudden third surgery. This surgery was to remove all the stitches from the second surgery.

After the surgery I learned that he could not be stitched up again. Once a wound like that is open again, the risk of infection is too high. He was sent home a few days later with a wound VAC. A wound VAC is a cumbersome battery-operated vacuum that sucks fluid from a sponge system taped to the opening in the skin until the skin grows enough for the wound to close on its own. He could not go anywhere without taking the VAC with him. We couldn't stay anywhere very long, or we'd have to find an electrical outlet to plug him into. He had to wear the wound VAC for almost two agonizing months.

The spongy dressing had to be changed three times a week, and each session took about an hour because of the length and depth of the incision. I can still remember the nurse saying, "It's a pretty wound, Mr. Vinnie, a pretty wound." What? Pretty? It was interesting maybe, but pretty? Only a nurse could say that. There was nothing pretty about it. It was painful. It was cumbersome, and the wound VAC made so much noise at night that we were often awakened by its gurgles and bubbling sounds. It was like having someone trying to start up an old car right in the bedroom.

Winter is always a hard season for me. I don't like cold weather. I don't like days of less sunlight either. That winter was the longest and most agonizing winter of my whole life (up until then). I had to learn to change an ostomy bag, and I had to take care of a very sick man who was always in pain. And in the midst of all this, my daughters were beginning to think they should bump their wedding dates up. There were so many things going on all around me that it made my head spin.

I had started a new job just before Vinnie got sick. We had to adjust to the fact that Vinnie would not get a reconstructed bladder. I was now a nurse at home, still taking care of the home, working outside the home, and trying to accept that life for Vinnie and me would never be the same again, and on top of that, I was planning two weddings. I had no idea that January 31 would mark the beginning of so many twisted events that would not only change us forever but events that would become the end of Vinnie's life on earth just months later.

A Wedding and a Memorial Service

By March, Vinnie was off the wound VAC and he returned to work. He was referred to an oncologist sometime in March or early April. The oncologist investigated his health record and was alarmed. Vinnie's options for treatment were going to be a challenge; he was limited in the types of chemotherapy he could have. The fact that he had hepatitis years ago could cause liver shock if one type of chemotherapy was used. The fact that he had only one kidney presented a problem if the other type of chemotherapy was used. The latest CT scan showed no signs of cancer, so Vinnie and I opted to do nothing. We didn't see any reason to make other parts of his body sick when there was no evidence of cancer anymore at that point.

Early in the year we also pulled together plans for the wedding of my oldest daughter, Amy. We were busy putting flower arrangements together and sewing wildly. But in spite of Vinnie's good report from the doctor, he was still very tired and in continued pain—extreme pain. We thought he was still recovering from the extensive surgery he'd had in January. After all, getting all those organs out is no small thing.

He barely made it through the wedding that day without collapsing into a chair begging to go home. At this point, his only place of relief from pain was in a hot bath.

Soon after the wedding, we got the news that Amy was pregnant—with twins! It was exciting to think of having twin grandchildren! But her pregnancy was not an easy one. She had constant cramping and was oftentimes in paralyzing pain. In spite of several visits to the doctor and even a few trips to emergency rooms, no one could tell her what was causing the pain. By the time it became apparent, it was too late.

She had been taking Tylenol for the pain. Tylenol also brings down fevers. One morning she realized that she had a low-grade fever, so she decided not to take Tylenol until she could see if the fever would rise without it. It did. She was off to the ER again; this time it was because of the high temperature and a high white blood cell count. She was admitted and put on a monitor. It was also discovered that she was in labor. At seventeen weeks, she would lose the babies if the infection causing the fever threw her body into labor.

The doctor quickly started an IV with high doses of antibiotics, but it was too late. In spite of the antibiotics, her water broke, and the babies were born around 1:30 in the morning. They were alive when they were born, wiggling in her hands, but they died while she was holding them. They never had a chance. I don't know if I was sadder for my daughter's loss or mine. It was one of the saddest days of my whole life, at least up that point.

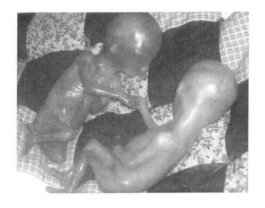

Amy was allowed to keep the babies with her in the hospital until she and her husband felt ready to say good-bye and let them go. The staff was very sensitive to their need to have closure. We gave Logan and Lauren a memorial service that Thursday.

The very next day after the memorial service for the twins, we had the rehearsal dinner for the wedding of my youngest daughter, Michelle (we call her Shelly). Oh my…what a month! Vinnie had another CT scan that week too; it came back clean. There were no signs of cancer. We could move on to happier events. Looking back on it, I can see that God did not allow us to see the cancer that I believe was still in there lurking and growing in Vinnie somewhere. God wanted us to marry our daughter without thinking he would not live much longer. Now that is grace! I was so amazed at God's loving kindness through this completely chaotic season of our lives.

Due to some scheduling conflicts, Shelly's rehearsal and rehearsal dinner had to be scheduled the week before the weekend of her wedding. (I highly recommend this. It gives a lot more time to rest before the wedding and takes a lot of stress off of the two affairs when they are back to back.) Shelly was getting married on our twenty-fifth wedding anniversary. She would carry on the tradition of celebrating her marriage on our date.

Because it was our twenty-fifth, we incorporated the event into Shelly's ceremony by renewing our vows first. We each wrote our own vows to each other and kept it a secret. Only Shelly and our pastor knew what we each had written, so it was interesting, to say the least, that we each said something about keeping our vows for "as many more days that the Lord would allow us to remain together." No one probably noticed, but even in that intimate moment of exchanging vows with the love of my life, it caught my attention. I couldn't help but wonder if Vinnie felt like I did… that our time wasn't going to be much longer. But I never asked him. In spite of the recent good diagnosis, I just sensed he knew too. I was more right than I could have imagined I'd be. I never wanted to be more wrong about something in my whole life.

Love Is Patient, Love Is...

Scripture is so convicting. I've heard that passage at just about every wedding I've ever attended: "Love is patient, love is kind. It does not envy, it does not boast, it is not proud" (1 Corinthians 13:4).

After Shelly's wedding, Vinnie and I took a little vacation in the mountains of Tennessee. We never made it to Alaska like we'd talked about for years before. It was our dream to go to Alaska for our twenty-fifth anniversary. We never got there. I joked that in Tennessee we'd still get to see mountains and water, but I was silently disappointed. Our dreams were fizzling away like smoke. But Vinnie was in so much pain and so exhausted from two weddings and so many months of pain. There was no point in going to Alaska (and no money to go, anyway). He slept most of the time we were away. He had little energy to take walks or even take a drive through a natural park. I did all the driving to Tennessee and back. It was a lonely vacation for me, really. When he was awake, he was uncomfortable and struggling with agonizing pain.

It didn't make sense to me that he was supposed to be cancer-free because he seemed to be more uncomfortable every day. He was taking strong pain medicine, but it never seemed to help. The pain medicine also caused him constipation, and constipation caused more pain. He asked me about every hour (I am not exaggerating!), "What should I do now? Take more pain medicine or a stool softener or a laxative?" It required so much patience!

Wow, I really needed that passage—daily! Love, love, love…is what? Oh yeah, patient and kind. Talk about a need for God to take over! He has the love; He has the patience. I needed His, for mine was wearing thin even though I did love him. This is the struggle of a selfish person who experiences the daily wrestling between the Holy Spirit, who can help us be like God, and the flesh that can make you feel like standing in the bathroom and screaming at the top of your lungs. I have a good friend who lives by the following words: "All for our good and His glory." I cherished those words and leaned on them to help me remember that God had a purpose even in all that.

Vinnie's pain continued to worsen every day, and every week he slept more than the week before, until he practically slept all the time. He would try to get up some mornings to go to work but would oftentimes call me an hour or two later with barely enough energy to speak. He'd tell me he could not make it through the day and was going home.

One day after being home all morning sleeping (pain kept him up for hours the night before), he attempted to go to work in the afternoon but ended up driving himself home around 4 p.m. (I did most of driving those days because he was too uncomfortable to drive). We were in the middle of a torrential rainstorm when I suddenly heard a car horn. I thought someone's horn was stuck. I looked outside and found Vinnie doubled over the steering wheel of his truck with his head on the horn.

I ran out to see what he was doing. He told me to call 911. He felt like his stomach was about to explode around the area of the stoma. He was scared, and he thought he was going to pass out. We went to the ER via ambulance and spent a good portion of the night there, but no one could figure out what had happened to him or what was wrong. Once again, I knew in my heart that the cancer wasn't gone at all. I sensed that the cancer was lurking around like a prowling lion, silently and secretly devouring little pieces of Vinnie every day.

Watching Vinnie was getting more and more scary every day. His behavior and ability to function was becoming more and more unreliable. I think it was another week or two before we discovered that the cancer was back. It was not a surprise, but it was terribly disappointing, defeating, and sad.

It was a Sunday morning. Vinnie was in bad shape, barely able to walk. We went to church (Vinnie was going places in a wheelchair at this point) and left immediately after the sermon. He was going to meet his son and son-in-law at the home of a friend to show them what needed to be done to finish a ceramic tile job he'd been doing for her. With Vinnie out of work so much, we were not getting his full paycheck. The side job was vital for us to pay for all the doctor visits, evenings in the ER, and the many, many prescriptions. He was supervising this tile job because he was in no condition to do the work.

That afternoon, while trying to show the boys what to do, he laid on the floor curled up in a ball in pain. My stepson finally called me and said, "You've got to take him to the hospital. Something's terribly wrong. He's in too much pain." Once again we were back in the ER.

This time when the doctor in the ER saw how much pain Vinnie was in, he knew Vinnie would have to be admitted to manage his pain. He was given several shots of morphine, and it was the first time in a long time I'd seen Vinnie seem himself again, with no pain! With the pain now under control, the doctor took measures to figure out what was causing all the pain. The first order of business was to get another CT scan.

He was admitted, and I went home to get a little sleep. I was to bring back fresh clothes for Vinnie to wear home in the morning. But I no sooner got home that evening than Vinnie called me. His doctor came to his room around 11:30 p.m. to tell him the results of the CT scan. The cancer was back. It was in the liver and lungs, traveling to the other kidney, as well as all over the lymph nodes in the back. I drove right back to the hospital. We talked, and though we had been somewhat preparing our hearts all these months in case we heard the word *terminal*, we still cried together for hours that night. The nurses let me stay in the extra bed in his room, and I stayed until morning.

His oncologist came in the morning to talk to us both. We were told that the cancer was aggressive and that he would get Vinnie set up for chemotherapy, but there was no question that Vinnie was going to die. The doctor knew that he would not be able to save Vinnie but hoped he'd be able to give him two or three more years to live. It took another five days before the doctors were able to get the right combination of pain medications to control the pain. Once they had the formula, Vinnie went back home to begin the new and what would be the last phase of his experience with cancer.

Shortly after he went home, we made a number of trips to the doctor's office to prepare for chemotherapy, but each time, there was a hitch. The creatinine count in the kidney was too high to do chemotherapy successfully. The creatinine is a measure used to determine how well the kidney is draining. Vinnie's kidney wasn't functioning well enough to withstand the stress from the chemotherapy. He was sent home several times. After many days of this, we were getting frustrated and tired.

After a few weeks of waiting and praying and hoping for the creatinine count to drop, the doctor decided Vinnie should have yet another operation. He wanted to open the ureter with a stint to get the kidney draining better, but the doctor performing the surgery realized halfway through the procedure that there was no blockage. The high creatinine count was now a mystery because it was obviously not caused by a kidney blockage. He was taken out of OR and sent home. Talk about patience. We were both being asked to have so much of it. We were both becoming worn out and ready to stop. A week later, we finally made that choice.

Celebration-of-Life Party: " We'll See You Later"

When Vinnie and I went to our last visit to the oncologist's office, we agreed that if the creatinine count was still high, we were not going to keep trying to get treatment for Vinnie. We were tired of the running around back and forth from one doctor's office and hospital to another. We were tired of all the disappointments, the pain, and the exhaustion of the whole experience. After all, didn't the doctor say he was going to die anyway? If the doctor was going to give him two or three more years, we certainly didn't want them to be like this! He wanted to die at home. All that running around was wearing us out, and he wasn't able to spend time with his family.

We arrived at the office. The nurses took blood to check the creatinine count. The doctor finally came in with the results of the blood test. His creatinine count was higher than ever before. This was the straw that broke the camel's back. We knew right then that we were at the end. We had a long talk with the doctor that morning. We were ready to do whatever it would take for Vinnie to simply die gracefully and in the comfort of our home, surrounded by his family.

The oncologist had us talk to the woman in charge of the hospice group at Duke right away. She just happened to be in the room next door that particular morning. After talking to her, we felt sure we were doing the right thing and had made the right choice. The doctor guessed that Vinnie would have two months to live. His guess was pretty darn close. Vinnie lived seven more weeks.

We received hospice care right away. Once a person starts hospice care, there are no more doctors. The nurses are no longer focused on making the patient live longer; they are focused on making him or her as comfortable as possible to travel the process of dying. Vinnie was really going to die, soon. I was sort of prepared, but it also seemed surreal. This couldn't really be happening, could it?

Back in March, shortly after Vinnie got off the wound VAC, I was in church one morning by myself (Vinnie wasn't feeling well that morning), and I felt like God told me that Vinnie was going to die before my fifty-second birthday. I believed he would die in August. So even though I felt hopeful all along, I also knew that those August days could be his last days on earth. Also in March, I attended the memorial service of a sweet friend's mother. Various family and friends stood up and shared a memorable moment about her during that service. I thought to myself then that if we were told that Vinnie would die, I'd throw Vinnie a party to celebrate his life so he could go home knowing how much his life meant to so many people.

Vinnie's life was a life deserving of a celebration. Paul wrote in 2 Timothy 4:7, "I have fought the good fight, I have finished the race, I have kept the faith." Vinnie wasn't Paul, but he kept the faith, even during the painful season of suffering with cancer. He continued to give glory to God and sing His praise. When one finishes a race, it is deserving of a celebration. Vinnie would get to celebrate the running and finishing of his race with his brothers and sisters in Christ. I couldn't think of a more honorable way for the man to go.

Once we stopped running to doctors' offices and hospitals, we were able to observe just how quickly he was deteriorating. I began to realize that if we were going to throw a party, we needed to have it soon. A couple we were very close to at the time offered to put the party together for me. We decided on a potluck after church. We had the party on the first Sunday in August. I am so glad we decided to have it at the church and not at our house. There were at least 300 people there.

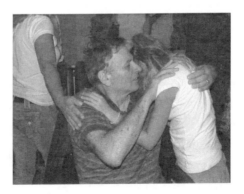

We started the party with one of Vinnie's favorite worship songs, "Here I Am to Worship." Then people were given a chance to get up to the microphone to share how much they loved Vinnie and/or how he had impacted their lives.

Many people could not get up and share. Their hearts were too broken. There was not a dry eye in the place that day. Vinnie was a well-loved man in the lives of many. I was proud to be his wife. The party ended when our worship leader sang "I Can Only Imagine." I wasn't sure he'd get through the song; it brought him to tears. It brought us all to tears. Vinnie was leaving us. He was going home, to heaven. We'd have to imagine it, but soon he would not be imagining it anymore.

After the party, many people knew it would be the last time they saw Vinnie. It took almost an hour for people to say good-bye to him that day. He lived three and a half weeks after that day and spent most of that time in bed.

It was puzzling to see a man with so much energy and so willing to drop anything and go help someone with a project so rapidly become weak and deteriorated, unable to walk, talk, and breathe as the cancer grew in his lungs. But Vinnie got to leave knowing that his life made a difference to others. He could leave with peace. We could let him go with peace of our own.

Cancer is a dreadful disease, but it does give us the time we need to say good-bye and let go of the one we love with peace and without regret. That part of cancer is a blessing. It's also a blessing because it gives everyone who is dying the chance to get his or her soul right with God. Vinnie's soul was right with God. We knew he was going to be Jesus in heaven very soon. I can't imagine how hard this journey would have been if we were not absolutely sure of that. Our time apart will only be a season, not forever. We will see him again in God's time.

The next two and a half weeks were busy—*very* busy! Our daughter Amy and her family moved into our house. Vinnie and I decided to take an apartment, where it was quieter and easier for me to care for him. Amy and her husband were going to rent our house when Vinnie passed because it was too big for me to take care of alone. It seemed a good idea at the time, and the hospice staff was very positive about it, so we did it. It was another episode of chaos, but we had dozens of people from our church help us move, pack, unpack, clean, and fix us meals. It was awesome.

As soon as we got in the apartment, visitors started coming. They came every day: people at the office, the church, and even from out of state. They came from New York. We got calls from people in Atlanta, Charlotte, and even Thailand! It was non-stop. Everyone wanted one last time or one last word with Vinnie.

Unfortunately, Vinnie didn't have much energy left at this point, but the calls and visits were closure for everyone. Every day he got closer and closer to death. I had wondered all along what it was going to be like one day if he would not survive this cancer, but this time I knew his time was near. I would sometimes watch him for hours in the night, wondering if I'd wake up in the morning and he'd be gone. He kept holding on. We kept holding on. Eventually the wait became agony for all of us (his family). But we tried to enjoy whatever bit of time we could keep with him. We didn't want him to leave, but we didn't want him to suffer anymore. We were ready to let him go.

At the Celebration-of-Life party we threw for Vinnie, people also had the opportunity to write their thoughts on cards so we could keep them forever to read. Our daughter Amy wrote a letter to her dad.

Near the end of the letter she said, "I'll never say good-bye to you, Daddy, never good-bye. I will only say, 'I'll see you later.'" The phrase "I'll see you later" became a cliché in the final weeks to come. It was our way of keeping the experience positive, and it was our way to still bring honor to Vinnie and glory to God.

"We'll see you later, Vinnie. We'll miss you, but we *will* see you later."

Lord, I've Changed My Mind!

While cancer was taking its inevitable course closer to Vinnie's death, it seemed that I was supernaturally and increasingly accepting of and preparing for the fate awaiting me in the weeks ahead. I was thinking positively about being single and serving God. I seemed to be content, even to my own surprise, with the road that was coming up over the horizon…that was, until the day Vinnie died. I woke up that morning with a sudden strange response to all that had been happening those past ten months with a plea to God: "Lord, I've changed my mind! I'm not okay with Vinnie leaving us. I'm not ready for him go! I've changed my mind!"

As Vinnie grew weaker and weaker in his last days, his pain medicine was increased each week, with it sometimes increased twice a week. He continued to "travel" daily. This is the description the hospice nurses give to Christians who are in the process of separating one's soul from being here to being in heaven. It's interesting that the nurses could actually see this difference. In fact, it seemed he was more "there" than here every day. He was eating less and less, and toward the end, it was even harder for him to drink any fluids. Sometimes he complained that his chest hurt, and he could feel the cancer choking his breath.

The Friday before he passed away, Vinnie's behavior was very peculiar. He seemed very restless that day and very uncomfortable that night when we went to bed. He kept getting up. He tried taking a hot bath, and he tried to rest on the floor, in his favorite chair, and in the chair with the massage cushion, but nothing worked. It kept me awake. He was not himself, and even his speech was not clear. It was getting harder and harder to understand what he was saying. I wondered if cancer was in his throat, preventing him from being able to speak.

I got up to see if I could help him. He got upset that I was "spying" on him. He wandered out of the apartment, but when he walked out on the porch, he stood still for a minute in his bathrobe, swaying back and forth. He finally came back inside and started staggering around the room, knocking things over and falling. He got hurt a few times. I thought he might fall and seriously injure himself, break something, or hurt someone in the house. I called the hospice nurse.

She told me he was experiencing terminal agitation. She said not everyone experienced this, but it was not uncommon. She reminded me that this behavior was an indication that he probably only had a day or two left to live and that nothing I could do at this point was going to hurt Vinnie. She then gave me a whole list of things to do to try to calm Vinnie down. I started giving him morphine every fifteen minutes, along with other medications that are supposed to calm a person down. I had to give it all to him in a syringe because he could not swallow very well.

I called her another hour or so later and told her that it wasn't helping; it was making him worse! She gave me another regimen of things to do and said that if I had to call her again, she would not hesitate to just come here from one hour away. I told her I'd try the next set of things to do. I didn't want her to come. It was already 1:00 a.m. However, when Vinnie started spitting the medication at me, I called and said, "Come! Please, just come!" She arrived an hour later.

When she arrived, I had already called 911, as she instructed. We were going to take Vinnie to the hospital. He was out of control, and I was unable to help him. I knew that being at the hospital was going to make him upset. He didn't want to go back to the hospital. Sure enough, he became very angry that he was being dragged out of his apartment and strapped to a stretcher.

He tried to get out of bed dozens of times when we first arrived at the hospital. Because of his aggressive and unpredictable behavior, the doctor ordered a nurse to stay in the room with him around the clock. All the nurses insisted I go home each night and get sleep because I would need the rest "in the end," so I arrived each morning to see Vinnie and stayed all day in the room with him. I loved being there all day. I didn't want to be anywhere else.

It didn't take long before I could see the blessing in the long, drawn-out week of waiting. I was getting used to being home alone in the evenings, especially when it was time to go to sleep. God was giving me the chance to get used to being there without Vinnie. Isn't God so good? It was painful but also a blessing. I was adapting and preparing my heart and mind for a new life without my partner, without my best friend.

Each day at the hospital, I would talk to the CNAs that stayed with Vinnie around the clock, and of course, I got to know all the RNs on the oncology floor. As I told them stories of Vinnie and my life together, our family, and about all the ways God revealed His goodness to us even along the sad and crazy journey of Vinnie's cancer, they began to love Vinnie more every day. They felt like they knew him, and we were all about to lose a good friend. Some remembered him from other hospital stays and already loved him.

By Wednesday morning that week, I realized that even though we wanted Vinnie to die at home, God had a different and very intentional plan by leading us to the hospital instead. He wanted us to be where others would be blessed by the stories of His hand at work in our lives over the years. I could hardly wait to tell Vinnie what God showed me. I wanted Vinnie to know that God wanted him in the hospital, not at home, and we could trust His reasons. Though he was pretty much in a coma-like state, I hoped he would comprehend what I had to tell him. I think he did. He squeezed my hand when I reminded him that we always said we wanted God's will over our own. That meant even about how and where he would die. He was calmer after that.

Each of the children had made a promise to Vinnie before he died. Each one's promise was different and pertinent to their own personalities and needs. One promised to be a peacemaker in the family. Another promised to finish school and position herself in a situation where she didn't have to rely on other people for basic survival anymore. I recently learned that even my sister and her husband made a promise to Vinnie. They promised to look after me for him.

I am not sure what two of our kids promised him, but I was well aware that I hadn't promised him anything. I felt like I should have something to promise him but didn't know what would be significant to him. I had given much thought to this over his last weeks, but it wasn't until that morning, that last Wednesday, that I realized why God might want him in the hospital in his last week and not at home. As I told him my revelation about why God wanted him in the hospital that last week of his life—that it was for the purpose of telling our story, God's story, and blessing others— it became apparent what my promise needed to be. I promised him that his death would not be in vain and that the story of our lives and God's work in our lives and in his journey of cancer and death would live on and bless others for years to come. I promised him I'd make sure of it.

It's not that I really wanted him to die, but every day I hoped would be his day home. It was so hard to see this strong, once-vibrant man melt away in a mindless state of sleep. I wish I could have turned back the hands of time and done something differently so he might have lived until we were both old and gray. I wish I'd spent more time with him in his last weeks instead of letting so many others see him, only to find that in my week with him, he would be in a coma. I wish holding onto him tightly would have kept him here with us for as long as I am to be on earth, but I knew it would not keep him here; it would just make us both more heartbroken about our time coming to an end.

His destination was clear that day. It was more important for Vinnie to know that I was going to be okay. I knew if there was anything I should cling to, it should be God's Word that tells us that our days are numbered. God's Word tells me that He predetermined when Vinnie would be finished running the race here, just as He has already determined what day I too will exit here and come home. I could trust His sovereign plan, because all of these days fit perfectly into God's redemptive big story.

That fine sunny Wednesday morning while I was telling Vinnie, again, that it was a perfect day for him to die, he seemed as though someone else were in the room talking to him in that moment, reminding him of what day it would be. I spoke; he turned his head slightly in the opposite direction and gave a subtle nod in agreement to what seemed to be an invisible someone speaking to him. I am now convinced that he was told that that Wednesday was not the perfect day but that the predetermined day that he would go home would be two days later: Friday. When Friday came, it became obvious for many reasons just what a perfect day it was.

That Wednesday I had a good day with Vinnie. I had a good conversation with the nurse on duty. I had a chance to talk to Vinnie without sensing he was mad at me for taking him to the hospital, where he would die. He chose hospice care so he could die at home. Vinnie seemed to be very calm and peaceful that day. I decided to stay that night in the room with him, and I stayed the next day, Thursday, until about 3:00 p.m.

At that point, I felt the need to go home, pay some bills, clean, and do some laundry. I called the hospital again around 9:00 p.m. His condition was the same. He was peaceful and resting. I decided to stay home and go to bed early. The hospice nurse did not tell me that the caregiver of a dying person oftentimes gets a sense of "housekeeping" like Vinnie had the week before, when the time is near, but Thursday became my housekeeping day; Vinnie died the next day.

I woke up at four o'clock that Friday morning of August 29, 2008, and couldn't go back to sleep. I called the hospital. The nurse reported once again that Vinnie was still the same. But I felt unexplainably dismal and somber that morning. The optimistic woman I'd been on this ten-month journey was suddenly slipping away with grief and the sudden realization that her/my life was about to change. I was about to lose my husband, who was a good man to my family, the community, and me. The reality of knowing that Vinnie was going to die soon suddenly stung deep in my soul like frozen sleet on cold cheeks.

I was overwhelmed by the thought of his leaving; it would be so final. I cried out to God and told him I was a fake. I told him I had only *thought* I was strong, but I wasn't. I told God that I had changed my mind! I didn't want Vinnie to leave us. I was not *really* okay with God's will in this matter. I told God that I still wanted to take pictures with Vinnie from the Alaskan cruise line we were supposed to go on. I reminded God that Vinnie and I had plans with our grandchildren and even our great-grandchildren. We'd planned also on someday buying an RV to sightsee and do ministry work in communities around the country. I didn't want Vinnie to go now, not now, not yet. I wasn't ready.

I knew my pleading wasn't going to change the facts. Vinnie was going to die. We would never travel in an RV. We'd never make it to Alaska. The only place we'd end up together now would be heaven, and he was going to be there soon. I was not.

As I was weeping, I suddenly looked in my bedroom and declared my peace with God, saying, "If you are going to leave me here without him, this bedroom has to become mine, not ours." I then proceeded to rip all the bed linens off the bed and threw them in the guest room. Before I went to the hospital that morning, I bought new linens with a gift card a friend had given me and put the new set in the trunk of my car.

When I arrived to the hospital parking deck, I received a surprising call from the charge nurse asking when I was going to be arriving to see Vinnie. I asked if Vinnie was still alive. She said he was but would talk to me more about his condition when I was on his floor. When I got off the elevator, the charge nurse greeted me at the elevator door and wrapped her arms around me. She told me with tears in her eyes, that "Mr. Vinnie" was having trouble breathing and that he was going to die in the next couple of hours.

When I entered his room, I realized that I was standing in our last few moments together. I called our daughter Shelly first, because she lived the farthest way, about an hour-and-a-half drive. She left right away and arrived at the hospital in record time in spite of heavy morning traffic. I called our oldest daughter, Amy, next. I knew she would have to find someone to watch her children, but ironically, her husband had just arrived home after being turned away at his place of employment due to the lack of work that day. He watched the children, and Amy was able to arrive at the hospital in just fifteen minutes (normally a thirty-minute drive).

I wanted to be with Vinnie in his final hour, and I wouldn't have traded that time with him for anything, but it was very hard (though also surreal). He had had the hardest time breathing. His frame was emaciated from lack of food and basic deterioration. His stomach sunk deep into the cavity of his torso. He looked so small and frail. I think I stroked his hair a million and a half times. I told him that he was the love of my life. I told him I'd changed my mind about him going home to heaven and that I wasn't okay with him leaving us. I told him I wished it could have been me that had been sick instead of him so he could stay here with his children and grandchildren. I told him I loved him and would never be the same without him. But in spite of all this dialogue of hope, I knew he was really going to die in these moments we stood over his failing body.

In his last few minutes, he was gasping for air. He would take a breath, and it would be another long and agonizing thirty or forty-five seconds, and he'd take another one. When it was clear that he'd taken his last breath, I noticed that his heart was still beating. It nearly killed me to watch it beating away and he wasn't breathing. It was awful. I put my hand over his heart until it didn't beat anymore. We each suddenly fell apart.

There were no nurses in the room in his final hour. A nurse did open the door at the end, and I whispered that Mr. Vinnie had gone home. She left the room. They gave us our time with him. His fight was over. He was with the Lord. I couldn't believe it was so final. I just couldn't believe it. I had changed my mind, but God had not changed His. Vinnie was gone from this life with us—gone. We were supposed to say, "I'll see you later," but it sure felt like "good-bye" to me.

Vinnie's daughter Christine was scheduled to close on a new house, their first home, that day with her husband. I told her to go to the closing knowing that her dad was proud of them. He would not have wanted her to postpone the closing. Vinnie died around 11:30 a.m. She arrived after the closing, around 1 p.m. Michael, Vinnie's son, was working out of state that day, but he was able to arrive at the hospital in Raleigh in just four hours. Christine was excited that she got to close on her house before her daddy died, just as she had hoped. She proudly brought the closing papers to the hospital with her. God's timing in all of it was perfect.

Finding My New Identity

The following evening was the showing at the funeral home. There were so many people at the funeral home that they were literally lined up outside the door. Some came from over two hours away to pay respects and condolences that evening. Just as many filled the church the following day, and though the memorial service was the saddest day that I'd ever experienced, I was comforted by the number of people who were concerned and desired to help in some way.

As prepared as I was for Vinnie's death, I had no way of knowing the intense feelings of sadness I would feel that day. He was to be cremated, but he was brought into the worship center of our church in a coffin and given a proper military service. At the moment that his body was carried out of the building to return to the funeral home, it felt like a piece of my heart was being torn right out of my chest cavity. My hand reached out as if to touch him one more time, and as I watched him slowly slip out of my sight, I almost fell to the ground. Being surrounded by loved ones was comforting and a distraction, but once I was home at the end of that day, the reality of Vinnie's permanent exit from our life here on earth was like a sword slowing sinking through every fiber of my being.

The weeks rolled almost without notice. Those first several weeks were a blur, but two months after Vinnie's final day on earth, my stepson Michael unexpectedly died.

I've heard some say that a spouse of many years may die shortly after their late spouse dies and the cause is from a broken heart. Though the autopsy report showed some health issues, I knew deep down in my heart that Michael died of a broken heart. He loved his dad dearly and couldn't come to grips with his death.

Again there was a short-lived crowd of friends to comfort us, but a few weeks later, the loneliness set in. There were fewer phone calls; the grandchildren and the girls went back to school and work. Friends and other family members returned to their families. I found myself so unexpectedly alone. It felt like I was suddenly standing in a large auditorium once filled with people who were evacuated while I made a quick trip to the restroom. I understood that everyone else had lives to return to and a normalcy to cling to, but not me. I was beginning to realize that I didn't have a life anymore. The life I knew with Vinnie was gone, and there was no other life I was prepared to live.

I began to realize that I had quite a bit of security stored up in these two men in my family, Vinnie and then Michael. After Vinnie died, I was comforted by the thought that Michael would help me if I needed it; it cushioned the blow of not having Vinnie in my life anymore. Michael's absence from my life removed the cushion. I was slipping on thin ice, and the water below was a chill to the bone. Their deaths were so final.

Mikey, as we called him, went out of his way to help his dad and sisters over the years, and he would have done almost anything to help me too. In fact, he was supposed to come to my house the day after his death. We were going to get the laminate flooring Vinnie bought for the old house and bring it to my new house (I bought a small home near my sister shortly after Vinnie died). Michael was going to lay the flooring for me and show me how to do it so I could help. I was looking forward to his company. I was sad that this project might never happen.

There were people who said they'd help me do any-thing, but I wondered if they really meant "anything." I just couldn't picture people dropping everything in their lives to come help me. I know that people *wanted* to help, but when it came right down to it, their lives were already full with dance lessons, sports, events to attend, errands to run, meetings to gather in, home-work to help with, weekends to spend together, or get-ting away on a date with their spouse. After all, I was once married for twenty-five years. I knew how it was.

It was clear; I was the one who didn't have a life. I realized my desperate need to make a life for myself, a new life, possibly with new friends that didn't have to be available for their husbands and children. I felt the need for a life that wouldn't cost anything either, because there was nothing extra in my modest budget to spend on a hobby or special monthly event. Life was looking quite bleak. *How does one make a new life at the age of fifty-two?* I wondered.

I was not really feeling sorry for myself. I was instead wondering what on earth my life was supposed to look like now. I was swimming around in dark water; it felt like I was drowning. I could hardly see anything around me. I could see that I had put too much stock in thinking that my life would always include Vinnie, the life we had together, and the direction our lives seemed destined to take. I wanted my life to have purpose again but could only tread uncharted waters. I had no idea where I was going or what I was doing.

I would often think of Job (name rhymes with robe) in the Old Testament. Job has his own book in the Bible. He was a righteous man and a wealthy man with a large family and many servants. Satan tells God that Job would not be a righteous man if all his wealth and belongings were taken away. God knows Job's faith would never allow him to be less in character even if his wealth, family, and belongings were taken away. When Satan asks, God allows all of Job's family to die and property to burn to the ground. The story ends when Job is reminded that God is the one who knows what He's doing. Job's faith skyrockets in chapter 38. When Job stands victorious over Satan's unseen battle, Job's health is restored, he is given a new family, and his wealth and assets become more than his previous worth.

I often wondered what Job thought when he lost all his children. My losses and grief were nothing compared to losing everything as he did, and I will leave a legacy of faith behind quite like Job's, but my desire was to get to the other side of this horrific year as if I were to be written in the hall of faith. Of course, I had no idea how I'd get to the other side, but I didn't want to waste time by asking "Why?" questions. I didn't want to ask, "Why me, Lord? Why Vinnie? Why now?" or "Why this way?" I had more important questions to ask, like, "How will I have enough money to live on when I don't make much money? How will I juggle the tasks of two people now that I'm the one left behind? How will I survive without someone to bounce ideas off of?"

I had many questions for God. I never questioned His sovereignty and His plan for my life, even now that Vinnie was no longer with me, or that God would somehow use these sad and tragic events for His glory and my good. Instead, I questioned if I'd ever see past my grief to recognize the next chapter that God desired for my life. I questioned whether I'd ever be strong enough to get through a day without weeping in public and wailing when I was alone. I wondered if I'd ever have the clarity to see beyond my broken heart and my sorrow and know what it might mean to heal.

In Job's story, there were children again and a restoration of wealth ten times the value of his loss. I was not sure if God would restore what I'd lost, but I knew, like Job, God knew more than my finite mind could ever comprehend. I needed to wait on God, for I knew He had something else in store for me. While waiting on God was very difficult, I instinctively knew that I had to go through the deepest pit of sorrow first. I had to acknowledge and accept the sense of emptiness and turn it over to God. He was the only one who could fill this enormous hole in my heart.

Two weeks after Vinnie's death, I began attending a Christian grief support group called GriefShare at a local church. I learned that there are many layers of grief. To truly heal from grief must slowly happen one layer at a time, not one layer skipped over to avoid the pain of it. There were many layers to face immediately. I missed Vinnie's company and his encouragement. I missed his phone calls every morning at work where he was simply telling me to have a wonderful day and reminding me that he loved me. I missed the quiet moments where we shared our hopes and dreams for the future and the concerns of the day at hand.

As I would sit in front of a mountain of receipts on the table and stare at bank statements that were months behind in being reconciled, I'd miss the bookkeeper. As I'd stare at the soiled carpets of my newly purchased home, I miss the handyman. When I walked on the vinyl floors in the kitchen, I'd think of all the friends who walked on tile that Vinnie had carefully laid in their kitchens and bathrooms and miss the ceramic tile man. They would walk on a memory of Vinnie for as long as they remained in their homes. I never would again. I was missing layer after layer of the onion of grief. Onions stink!

My desperate, floundering state of searching for some kind of normalcy in life again led me to call on and rely on God like never before for every single thing—even things that were easy and simple to figure out before. I began to realize that if I'd relied on God this much before Vinnie died, I might not be at such a loss for existence now that he was gone. I began to realize that with each layer of grief I had to face was also a new layer or depth of dependency God wanted me to experience with Him. His grace allowed me to understand new layers of the relationship God desired to have with me—one step, one layer at a time.

Survival now came mostly by journaling and praying—for daily bread, for protection, for joy (what little I might experience again), for peace, for security—for *everything*. It seemed I could no longer do even the simplest things anymore. Winter was approaching. It was a time for old things to die and wait for the springing forth of new life to come in its season. It was in the waiting on God, the desperate prayers, that I discovered God, my Maker, not only as my loving Father but also my perfect husband.

Part Three:

God as Our Husband
(Unraveling Isaiah 54:5)

Our Maker

For your **Maker** is your husband—the
Lᴏʀᴅ Almighty is his name—the Holy
One of Israel is your Redeemer; he is called
the God of all the earth.

Isaiah 54:5

God is our Maker. He created each of us. Genesis
1:26 says, "Then God said, 'Let us make man in our
image, in our likeness, and let them rule over the fish
of the sea and the birds of the air, over the livestock,
over all the earth, and over all the creatures that move
along the ground.'" He made each one of us with a
unique blend of His multifaceted aspects of Himself,
His character.

One weekend Vinnie and I went to a marriage
conference. There were many sessions throughout the
weekend that involved the entire group that attended.

After each session, we had to go off by ourselves and write a letter to our spouse. We were given a specific topic to address for each letter and a specific amount of time to write it. At the end of each writing session, we were to read the letters to our spouses. One couple hated the exercise and left early. The rest of us complained about all the writing for the few sessions but then began to see something amazing. We were beginning to realize that we assumed our spouse knew a lot more about us than they really did! For Vinnie and me, learning new things about each other helped us fall in love all over again.

Raising a family, tackling financial solutions, experiencing work and family stresses, completing mundane daily chores, and even maturing can add to the things that change about us as we travel from one year to the next with our loved ones. Vinnie and I were surprised at how we had changed concerning what we hoped to do in the future. The hopes we had for our children and the desires we had for a home, cars, and travel when we were to become empty nesters had all changed with new seasons in life. Our American dream changed over time. If Vinnie were still alive and I could know what I know now, my dreams for us would be different still.

The amount of work it would take for two people, no matter how close they may be, to talk about every thought, every dream, every idea, every attitude, every ache in the heart, or worry in the mind is impossible to tackle. I do know of marriages where the spouses know a whole lot about their mate, but to know every single little thing is not humanly possible, even for the best of couples. But it's not impossible for God to know every single little thing about us. In fact, God probably knows more about you than you do! And why wouldn't He? He made us.

If you make a cake from scratch, you can probably rattle off exactly what you put in the batter when your friends ask for the recipe. You remember every ingredient you put in. You know exactly all the quirks that it took to get the task done. You might even have some funny stories to tell about a time when you added salt instead of sugar or fished for a broken eggshell for twenty minutes before baking a delicious cake. Different factors can make the cake come out slightly different from one time to the next. Factors such as filtered, well, or city water, humidity, and altitude can affect each one's cake differently, even though the recipe might be the same.

God made each one of us completely unique compared to any other. He knows *every* single thing about you—everything! Even the hairs on our heads are numbered, according to Jesus Himself in Matthew 10:30. And He's had every ingredient in mind since before we were born, knitting us in our mother's womb, as it says in Psalm 139:13. But this passage in Isaiah 54 says that our Maker, who knows everything about us, is also our husband! That is remarkable! No human being has ever known or understood every single thing about us or understood every single need we have. But our heavenly husband who is also our Maker does! He sees His bride, you and me, as beautiful, lovely, and perhaps even breathtaking, as implied in Revelation 21:2: "I saw the Holy City, the New Jerusalem, coming down out of heaven from God, prepared as a bride beautifully dressed for her husband."

If we have placed our faith and trust in God's Son, Jesus, God sees us prepared as a bride beautifully dressed for Him! I am not beautiful in the earthly sense (although my sweet Vinnie thought I was beautiful, gorgeous, and even sexy). But when my heavenly husband looks at me covered in the blood of His Son, Jesus, He sees me as one of His most pure and lovely women.

Your Maker is your husband. Do you know that? Do you claim that in your life? Does your life reflect that fact? Are you confident of this relationship when you arrive home at night to an empty home? Do you go to Him as a husband who understands every single little thing about you because He's also your Maker?

We do live in a broken world, and it's also important to recognize that while there is a "you" created by God, there is also a "you" that was created by other things—uncontrollable circumstances, fears, or consequences of your own sin or bad choices in your life. All these things shape the people we become along the journey of our lives. God knows every single aspect of this "you." He still loves you, but He also has a plan for you to become more like Him.

Ephesians 4:22-32 makes it clear for us that there is a sinful, deceitful nature about us that is not of God. It also makes it clear that we have characteristics of God within our personalities. The passage says:

> You were taught, with regard to your for-
> mer way of life, to put off your old self,
> which is being corrupted by its deceitful
> desires; to be made new in the attitude of
> your minds; and to put on the new self, cre-

ated to be like God in true righteousness and holiness. Therefore each of you must put off falsehood and speak truthfully to his neighbor, for we are all members of one body. "In your anger do not sin": Do not let the sun go down while you are still angry, and do not give the devil a foothold. He who has been stealing must steal no longer, but must work, doing something useful with his own hands, that he may have something to share with those in need. Do not let any unwholesome talk come out of your mouths, but only what is helpful for building others up according to their needs, that it may benefit those who listen. And do not grieve the Holy Spirit of God, with whom you were sealed for the day of redemption. Get rid of all bitterness, rage and anger, brawling and slander, along with every form of malice. Be kind and compassionate to one another, forgiving each other, just as in Christ God forgave you.

The key statement in this passage is in verses 22-24: "You were taught, with regard to your former way of life, *to put off your old self,* which is being corrupted by its deceitful desires; to *be made new* in the attitude of your minds; and to *put on the new self, created to be like God* in true righteousness and holiness." (emphasis mine) Here's the point: When we become followers of Christ, we are forgiven of our sins. We then begin a process of becoming less of the old self and allow God to bring forth the characteristics that are like Him.

Let me make the point here that the "old self" is not completely bad. There are thousands, if not millions, of good people in the world who are not believers in Jesus. However, even good people have sins that aren't always seen on the surface, even by the person himself. This might be you. We aren't all bad before we're Christ followers and then become good. We just aren't completely good or Godlike, but when we become Christ followers, we can become more like our Maker's image every single day. That's the point.

The passage gives us a pretty good start to the list of the characteristics and behavior that are not of God. The list includes falsehood, unwholesome talk, bitterness, rage, anger, brawling, slander, and malice. It's not hard for us to think of many other characteristics not listed here but that are also not of God. There's bragging, arrogance, pride, cheating, lying, gossiping, being lazy, lacking self-control, self-pity, self-hatred, idolatry, greediness, and hatefulness.

Unlike the characteristics of our personalities shaped by circumstances, emotions, and sin and consequences of our bad choices, we do need to turn to the Bible for a description of God's characteristics. We should want to know from God Himself who He is, and not describe God by who we want, wish, or think He is or should be. Though some of the characteristics listed below might be obvious to some, others may think of God as a mean bully or an angry figure. Read each one carefully. God is waiting for you to know that you were made in the image of each of these! This is not an exhaustive list.

- Be fruitful: "But the fruit of the Spirit is love, joy, peace, patience, kindness, goodness, faithfulness, gentleness and self-control" (Galatians 5:22-23a).

- Strength: "Though he stumble, he will not fall, for the LORD upholds him with his hand" (Psalm 37:24).

- Faith/optimistic: "He will have no fear of bad news; his heart is steadfast, trusting in the LORD" (Psalm 112:7).

- Content/steady: "My heart is steadfast, O God; I will sing and make music with all my soul" (Psalm 108:1).

- Able to persevere: "The LORD will fulfill his purpose for me; your love, O LORD, endures forever—do not abandon the works of your hands" (Psalm 138:8).

- Merciful: "For the LORD your God is a merciful God; he will not abandon or destroy you or forget the covenant with your forefathers, which he confirmed to them by oath" (Deuteronomy 4:31).

- Kindness: "In a surge of anger I hid my face from you for a moment, but with everlasting kindness I will have compassion on you," says the LORD your Redeemer" (Isaiah 54:8).

- Changeless/Steady: You will roll them up like a robe; like a garment they will be changed. But you [God] remain the same, and your years will never end" (Hebrews 1:12).

- Energetic/Strong: "Do you not know? Have you not heard? The LORD is the everlasting God, the Creator of the ends of the earth. He will not grow tired or weary, and his understanding no one can fathom. He gives strength to the weary and increases the power of the weak. Even youths grow tired and weary, and young men stumble and fall; but those who hope in the LORD will renew their strength. They will soar on wings like eagles; they will run and not grow weary, they will walk and not be faint" (Isaiah 40:27-31).

- Compassionate: "The LORD is good to all; he has compassion on all he has made" (Psalm 145:9).

- Wisdom: "If any of you lacks wisdom, he should ask God, who gives generously to all without finding fault, and it will be given to him" (James 1:5).

- Humility: "All of you, clothe yourselves with humility toward one another, because, 'God opposes the proud but gives grace to the humble'" (1 Peter 5:5).

- Gentle: "Be completely humble and gentle; be patient, bearing with one another in love" (Ephesians 4:2).

Now that we've examined carefully the characteristics of our sinful nature and God's image, it's time to look inside and take inventory of both the "you" God created you to be and who you've become as a result of your life journey. Take your time with this exercise and come back to it as new thoughts come to mind. Remember, there are no secrets with God, so go ahead and be honest. He already knows the answers before you do!

Before you begin, let me encourage you to pray. Ask God to help you think of the many layers that make you who you are today, to discern which of those layers were created by God and which are the result of living in a fallen world. Ask Him also to continuously remind you that in spite of the many layers of self that are not of His image and likeness, He still loves you. Let's pray right now that He will help you through this important exercise. Here's a prayer you might pray if you don't know where to begin:

> Heavenly Father, help me think clearly about who you made me to be. I know there are areas of my personality that are not of you. I know I am fearful sometimes. I worry; I am mean on occasion and sometimes look down on people. Show me why I am like this and show me how to let this part of me go

so I can shine as the woman you made me to be. I want to know the beautiful bride you know me as. I really need to know you as my husband, and I know that I will experience the sweet relationship you long to have with me if I become more and more the bride I'm meant to be. I pray you shine your brilliant light on my heart and show me areas of my life that you want me to let go of. I have such heaviness to carry now that I am alone. I need to let some of this go so I have the strength to carry the load that today brings. Be my husband, one who helps carry the load and even carries me when it seems I can't go on. I pray this in Jesus's name. Amen.

Think for a few minutes about how a sibling or your best friend would describe you to a stranger; what would you expect to hear him or her say about you? (She knows that you'll never know what she said, so she'll be telling all your traits—good and bad.) When some of these characteristics are fresh in your mind, begin writing them below. Be sure to write down characteristics of the past as well. For instance, you might have been shy or fearful at one time. Though it may seem that you're not like that anymore, there's a good chance that you are that way sometimes, so it's better to be thorough. You can come back and add more as thoughts come to you later.

_____

_____

_____

_____

_____

_____

_____

_____

_____

_____

_____

_____

Now that you feel you've exhausted the list (and you can come back to it anytime), let's go back and determine which of these characteristics, distinctive traits, or qualities are of God and who He created you to be, and which are products of circumstance. Go back through the list and put an *M* for "Maker" next to the characteristics God made. Put a *C* for "circumstance" and sin nature next to those listed that were created by our response to circumstances in life.

If we are to understand our Maker as our husband, it is vital that we begin the work of putting off and putting on. Look at your list of characteristics that were shaped out of circumstance and this sinful world. Which do you think God might want you to put off first? Put the numbers "1," "2," and "3" next to the ones that you believe God wants to you to begin putting off.

Of the characteristics of God listed in the verses above, which ones really stand out as the ones God wants to begin to strengthen in you? These may be characteristics described in the verses that didn't get written on the list you made describing yourself. For instance, you might feel as though God wants you to work on being more patient. If patience is not on your list, go ahead and include it now. Write the verse or verses describing the characteristics of God that have the greatest meaning to you on a separate piece of paper or index card, and post it where you can see it during the day (such as the refrigerator, dashboard, or framed on your desk or mantel).

We have discussed the characteristics of our personalities that were created by our Maker and others as products of our sinful world. We concluded that changing who we've been to who we were meant to be is a process of putting on God's character and putting off the old self-nature. Begin praying daily to put off the old and put on the new. Journal those times when you failed to put off an old part of yourself and include why you think you got tripped up or continue to get tripped up in that type of circumstance. Keep asking for God's help, and watch the change that takes place in the months ahead.

It doesn't happen overnight. Sometimes there are circumstances in our lives that create deep patterns or habits in our personalities that seem especially difficult to put off without help. Take a moment to consider the following questions: Do you hold a grudge or blame anyone in your life for ugly areas of your current personality? Do you deal with strong issues of anger or perhaps fear? Do you carry guilt and shame and find it difficult to accept Christ's forgiveness in this area of your life?

If the answer is yes, it is highly recommended that you find someone who can help you in this area. It might be a pastor, a counselor, or a lay leader in the church who will walk alongside you in this area. If you can't do it alone, you aren't meant to. That is one of the wonderful aspects of the church. We are here to help each other grow in spiritual maturity, which means we become more like our Maker every day.

God is our Maker; He is a Maker who knows every single thing about us—from what He put in the mix to what was thrown in from the world. Our Maker knows us through and through. He knows what will bring us the greatest joys in life better than we do, because He made us. He even has it in store for us before we ask or figure out we should! As you begin to allow God to put off that which was not in His original recipe for you and focus on bringing out or putting on that which is who He made you to be, you will begin to grow in your love relationship with Him. Your joy will not only begin to return, but it will begin to be complete.

Our Husband

> For your Maker is your **husband**—the
> Lord Almighty is his name—the Holy
> One of Israel is your Redeemer; he is called
> the God of all the earth.
>
> Isaiah 54:5

During the time that my late husband, Vinnie, and I were married, we had many dreams. We had plans, goals, and tasks we shared. In our marriage, Vinnie usually washed dishes, for instance, and while he was a wonderful cook and did cook once in a while, especially when we had company, I did most of the cooking and emptied the dishwasher. He washed dishes after dinner. I cleaned the house. He took care of all home repairs and car maintenance. I did most of the grocery shopping, although we loved to shop together (but when we did, we'd overspend). He did the book-keeping, and I took care of the kids' needs (pack backpacks, make lunches, that sort of thing), and I did the laundry.

I know you can relate to this. When we become widowed, we not only lose our lover, our soul mate, and our friend, but we also lose the one who helped get things done around the house and in the family. We lose a partner to help us make decisions. Our dreams for the future are shattered. Grief is hard enough in accepting that the person you have lived with for years and years is gone, but there are layers and layers of other losses when our husband dies.

One friend of mine describes the experience to wearing hats. We lose many hats we used to wear, like lover and confidant, and we put on hats we may have never worn before, like a mechanic or being single. While we grieve these losses, everything that had to get done before still has to get done (take out the trash, mow the lawn, cut the hedges, cook, clean—the list goes on). But now it is up to you to figure out how. It's difficult to figure all that out, especially when life goes on and on. Before you know it, chores are all piled up!

I wish I could tell you that God Himself would come down and cut that lawn of yours, but we both know it's not going to happen quite like that. However, I will tell you that God has a plan.

In section one we talked our Maker knows every single detail of how He made everything, but He is also God or Lord over every single thing too. If you are His bride, He already knows all the pieces missing now that your earthly husband is gone.

When I first read the passage in Isaiah, I remember asking God to show me how He could be possibly 'be' my Husband. My earthly husband did so much for our family and around the home. When he died, I didn't see how I could do it all alone. I would joke with people after Vinnie died, saying, "One man died, but it might take thirty to replace him."

It dawned on me one day that God, my heavenly husband, *could* have a plan to fill the roles once filled by my earthly husband—in practical ways. My thought was that if God knew I needed the help, He'd provide it. If He didn't provide it, then perhaps He had a different plan or direction for my life (like move to an apartment or rent a room somewhere).

I began to pray that God would bring me someone to help me with chores around the house. I literally had a young man come up to me in church one day

(I didn't even know his name at the time) and ask if I needed help with yard work. I had to admit that I needed help. He arranged to come every week to mow the lawn. Since he would come straight from work, I'd cook a meal for him before he'd get to the grass. This was a blessing to him because as a single college boy, he ate mostly fast food.

This is just like God! He had this young man in mind the whole time. I've since had dozens of people come help me paint my house, cut dead trees, fix screens, hang new fans, replace old outdoor lighting, and a myriad of other things. Two young men even came to lay wood flooring that my husband never got to put down, and they did three rooms free of charge. The next summer, the first young man was no longer available to help with the lawn. God instead orchestrated a situation where I'd be offered a riding mower for only $100. That year I was able to do the lawn myself.

In the overwhelming process of healing from such a significant loss as that of a spouse, it is helpful to take inventory of all the layers of losses. Make a list below of the different areas of your life where you miss the role of your partner. If you are listening to this on CD, give thought to this today and be ready to start the list below on the journal pages of the book. Take your time and come back to this list as each layer comes to mind. We will come back to this list later in our study.

Indoor chores:

_____

_____

_____

_____

_____

Yard and vehicle chores:

_____

_____

_____

_____

_____

Financial tasks:

_____

_____

_____

_____

_____

Other areas of the home, work, business, family:

_____

_____

_____

_____

_____

I am blessed with many friends, but I have no doubt that if you pray for help, God will provide even if you don't know many people or have family living nearby. The trick is to keep watching, not be afraid to accept help, and to even be brave enough to ask for it! If you find it difficult to ask people for help or you aren't comfortable telling people what you need, ask for an advocate, a friend who will write down all the things that you'd like help with. Share the list you created above with her. Have her find people to fill those needs. This works like a charm! If there seems to be no one to help (and be sure it's not just that you are not making the need known to others), then perhaps you can be asking God if He's trying to redirect your path so you'll have less to take care of. This entire process is one of asking, waiting, watching, and asking again about how God seems to be answering. Be patient and sure—God does have an answer for you!

At this point you may be wondering how God might fill the role that your husband filled in more intimate or less tangible ways. God may not audibly have conversations with us, and He's not going to climb into bed and rub His soft feet over ours either. But He does want to meet us for quiet conversations in a beach chair while waves wash over us. He'll meet you while you are in a chair, all wrapped up in a blanket. He'll meet you while you are weeping or wailing. He loves you and wants you to sense His presence and His love for you. Sometimes I put on soft music, close my eyes, and ask Jesus to hold me in his arms. I've pictured Him dancing with me in fields of soft grass, sitting in gardens full of flowers, and walking along edges of cliffs, admiring His beautiful creation. I know He is honored that I'd take time to see myself with Him like this. It's the best I can have of Him now, but I know the best will come in due time. I take retreats with my Jesus!

This is experiencing intimacy with God, but God also talks to us. We can know what He says to us by being in the Bible. Then there are times when we might hear or sense the need to be ready for something. For instance, about six months before Vinnie died, I sensed that Vinnie was going to die before my fifty-second birthday. Was I sure this was God? Not at the time, but when Vinnie died the week before my fifty-second birthday, I was so glad I had slightly prepared myself just in case. This sensing was part of God's provision for me. He was preparing my heart for Vinnie's death. That is my loving husband. It has taken fifteen years to develop this intimate relationship with Him. It doesn't come overnight. But just because the level of intimacy may deepen over time,

God's promise to provide does not. His promise is always faithful!

I've had to develop ears to hear him and recognize His voice. It's not audible to human ears, but is the whisper of a husband always audible? How many times did I *know* Vinnie was saying "You are the love of my life" when words never spilled out of his mouth? So it is with God, our Maker, our husband.

Our husbands also played roles in more intimate areas of our lives. Check off the other boxes that apply below. These may seem obvious, but it is important to keep each layer of loss separate to avoid becoming overwhelmed. Space is provided for you to include specific ways your husband played out each of these roles in your life.

____ Confidant

Though a confidant does not solve all problems, few inner secrets, problems, and affairs are kept private like those known and kept by a spouse!

_____

_____

_____

_____

_____

____ Lover

There's nothing like crawling into the arms of warm flesh, not only feeling warm skin of yours. This is often one of the hardest areas of widowhood to adjust to.

_____

_____

_____

_____

_____

____ Encourager

Was your spouse one who encouraged you to be who you are made to be? Do you miss having a live-in friend who gave you a boost each day when you needed it? My husband called me every morning at work just to say "good morning" and to encourage me as I started my day.

_____

_____

_____

_____

_____

_____ Advisor

My pastor has sometimes referred to me as an idea machine. If I didn't have my husband to advise me, I can't imagine how many pots I'd be stirring today!

_____

_____

_____

_____

_____

____ Accountability partner

A husband who's concerned for our spiritual growth will always help keep us in check, helping us keep our greatest heart's desire for things that are on the heart of God.

_____

_____

_____

_____

_____

____ Spiritual leader

I miss a built-in prayer partner. And if we didn't pray together on a certain day, I knew he always prayed for me. I miss also having someone to meditate on Scriptures with, keeping our life purpose on God.

_____

_____

_____

_____

_____

____Other(explain)_____

_____

_____

_____

_____

_____

It's my ultimate belief that experiencing God in these most intimate ways and places in our lives is the greatest experience God desires of us on this side of widowhood when our hearts ache most for our earthly husbands. Put a check mark next to the roles that you are missing now. Space is provided under each role to expand on and describe in more detail. Again, take time to pray over each of these roles, asking God how He desires to fill these in your life and be watchful for His answers. He may bring a new friend in your life or you become aware of Bible study in your community or a ministry to become involved in. Be sure of this. As you pray about these, God does have an answer, so listen carefully.

The last exercise in this section is to make a list of people in your life that you could ask to help you with certain tasks. When you've exhausted this list of all potential helpers, look at the tasks and roles you wrote down earlier in this section. Match some of the people on your list with some of those tasks. Ask them for help, or ask a friend to help you organize and recruit help from this list. Continue to ask for God's help in showing you who else He might send to help you. As you meet new people, write down their names and ask God if He sent any of them into your life to be of help somehow. Ask God to place people in your life that will help you. Then start watching and listening. When someone on this list helps, make a note on the list and thank God for His kindness. He'll show you. Let's pray together right now to help you begin this exercise.

Dear heavenly Father, my perfect husband, I am overwhelmed with the many things

I must take care of now. My responsibilities are great, and I find it difficult to think through all of this. I'm flooded with sorrow, and it's difficult to sort my thoughts. Please, Father, help me focus. Bring to mind all those you have surrounded me with, and show me who in my life you desire to help in this time of trouble. Give me wisdom, clarity, and discernment to know where to get help from and what tasks aren't important anymore that I need to let go of. Send me a special friend who can help me sort this out. I know you love me and have a plan for my life now that I'm no longer married—a plan that includes today and tomorrow. I pray in Jesus's name. Amen.

Begin your list of potential helpers.

_____

_____

_____

_____

_____

_____

_____

_____

_____

_____

I have a husband who's perfect, who knows me more than I know myself, who is never about His personal gain, who loves me beyond my wildest desires and sets me free from bondage to the things that would eternally destroy my chances of ever knowing Him. Women looking for a perfect husband will *never* find a human one here on this side of heaven! Some may come close, but for all the little ways he doesn't make the mark, there is the perfect One ready to fill our hearts in the sweetest ways. Every missing aspect of your earthly husband can be found in your heavenly one.

Bride of Royalty

For your Maker is your husband—the **Lord Almighty** is his name—the Holy One of Israel is your Redeemer; he is called the God of all the earth.

Isaiah 54:5

So the Lord is not only our Maker and our husband, but He is also almighty and powerful! You are the bride of royalty! Imagine for a moment being the wife of the president of the United States, one of the most powerful men on earth. Now imagine being the wife of someone even more powerful that. Imagine being the wife of the most powerful, the One whose name is above all others; He is so powerful that He oversees all things and all at the same time too. Now there's a powerful husband—and *you* are His bride.

Let me tell you that the wife of such a powerful man as the president of the USA is also pretty important. The first lady is a powerful, influential person just because she is the president's wife. Some first ladies might have been rather proud of themselves and their high esteem and influence, but as the bride of the King of kings, we must be humble yet confident in our role as His bride. It is only because of our husband that we have any influence in the world He's placed us in. Do you see yourself as being a powerful and influential woman because you are married to the One who oversees all things?

You play a role in the big scheme of things. Even while you are mourning and sorting out the hazy steps in your journey as a widow, there are people who are watching. Your faith in Christ during this time is a very powerful influence on others! It is very a powerful influence on others to be honest about the journey and while keeping the faith in Christ, be able to also express the struggles of the journey. Remember that struggling with God is not a lack of faith; it is an acknowledgment of His existence!

We must keep our faith real for the children or grandchildren in our families. Your faith also influences neighbors, friends, and extended family by your trust and faith in your husband, the King of kings. Your faith may influence many of them to seek Him in their own lives. It can be compared to being the first lady in election time. We want to give as many people as possible the opportunity to place their 'vote' (faith or trust) in Jesus because their eternal life depends on it. Even in your lowest moments, your faith in your husband can influence many others with an eternal destiny. That is pretty important!

You are just as vital as any leader over this country. We are not important in and of ourselves, but our husband is LORD Almighty. It's an honor to be His special beloved. As believers in Jesus Christ, we have the power within us to do all that Jesus did when He walked the earth. In fact, if we are believers, we are given power to do even more than He did. Jesus, in John 14:12, tells us, "I tell you the truth, anyone who has faith in me will do what I have been doing. He will do even greater things than these, because I am going to the Father."

Have you this kind of faith in Jesus? _____

If not, go back to the introduction section on what it means to become a believer in Jesus Christ.

If you are a believer, do you live with the recognition that you have been given such power just because of your relationship with your husband, the Lord God Almighty? _____

Before you begin this part of section three, please note that there is a normal period of time in the grief journey for grieving. This may accompany a lack of energy and even a lack of concentration. This section may be too much for you right now. Be encouraged to read through it, but also feel free to come back to it at a later time—perhaps several months from now. Remember that it's not important that you go through this book in a particular amount of time. It is for you to take inventory and evaluate what your needs are and what new direction God has for your life in this new season.

If you are ready to begin this section, let's begin with prayer.

> Heavenly Father,
> You made us each for a purpose. Each one of us is unique, and so is the call you have on our lives. A call is not just for missionaries, clergy, and teachers. Every child of God has a vital role to play in the big

scheme of things—your big picture of salvation on earth. Please, Lord, give me a clear mind to think through the areas of my life where I've believed something that is contrary to your Word. Give me your eyes to see those and myself around me with your heart of mercy, grace, and compassion. Give me wisdom to discern your will for my life both for today and for the days that lie ahead. I am trusting in you to show me, because I need to believe that you are very much alive and active in my life and have a purpose for my life now. Help me to comprehend just how valuable I really am to you and valuable to the people you have placed strategically in my world. Use me for your glory! I pray in Jesus's name. Amen.

What are some of the important areas of life that you believe Jesus has given you to have a powerful influence in? Let's look at some of the possible groups of people you influence in your life. Next to each group below, write the names of those who come to mind in that group.

Church community (such as youth, young believers, young mothers):

_____

_____

_____

_____

_____

_____

_____

_____

Community/neighbors (such as social, civil or activity clubs, school organizations, women or young people in your neighborhood):

_____

_____

_____

_____

_____

Immediate family (such as children and grandchildren, parents):

_____

_____

_____

_____

_____

Extended family (include in-laws):

_____

_____

_____

_____

_____

When we cannot see ourselves as having any meaning or purpose in the lives of others, we instead believe lies about what and who we are. In other words, we believe something other than what the Bible tells us is true about us. While it's true that we are no better than slime of the earth, in Christ we rise on wings like eagles (Isaiah 40:31). While it is true that we might be weak, in Christ we are made strong in our weakness (2 Corinthians 12:10). While we might have a past as dark as the deepest caverns of the earth, we are made clean in Christ. Second Timothy 20-21 tells us: "Those who cleanse themselves from the latter [old self] will be instruments for special purposes, made holy, useful to the Master and prepared to do any good work." Whatever we were before Christ no longer exists when we are in Christ! We are cleansed by Christ and then become a new creation (2 Corinthians 5:17). I love that 2 Timothy 2:21 tells us that when Christ cleanses us, it is for a noble purpose!

The first lady does many things while her husband is in office. She campaigns with her husband, hoping to win the votes of the American people for her husband's name and sake. She supports organizations and participates in charity work for the sake of her husband's good name. She sits with advisors and learns the proper way to conduct herself in her role, and she socializes with other leaders and their wives. This type of mentoring and accountability strengthens and encourages her to continue in her quest to enhance and accentuate the work of her husband.

As the bride of the almighty King of kings and Lord of lords, we can also be groomed to be the best bride possible. We can talk to others about our amazing husband and be sure that our lives reflect that relationship. We can seek God's will for our lives and learn how our gifts, talents, and abilities fit within the bigger body of Christ known as His Church. We can also attend Bible studies and sit under the teaching of godly women who can mentor us and teach us about what the Bible has to say about who God is and who we are in Christ. Attempting to help others and become who we are meant to be, pointing to our heavenly husband even in the midst of the rocky journey of widowhood, will in fact help us in the healing process. Remember to take your time with this exercise and come back to it periodically to add to it or to see the progress you're making!

Are there women in your life that are
mature in their relationship with the Lord
that you can go to for prayer and encouragement? If so, who are they?

If you answered no, ask God to show you who He might have placed or is placing in your life now to help you develop your role as the bride of Christ. Write down anyone who might come to mind.

_____

_____

_____

_____

_____

_____

_____

_____

_____

_____

_____

Jesus is also our High Priest. As His bride, you are also a priestess, which is like the status of royalty. I love the beautiful words spoken by Peter in 1 Peter 2:5: "You also, like living stones, are being built into a spiritual house to be a holy priesthood, offering spiritual sacrifices acceptable to God through Jesus Christ." And verse 9 says, "But you are a chosen people, a royal priesthood, a holy nation, a people belonging to God, that you may declare the praises of him who called you out of darkness into his wonderful light."

Believers are "being built," "chosen," and "rescued from darkness" to praise Him and live in His wonderful light. When people meet you, is it clear to them that you are working on your marriage to the Lord Almighty? Let's look at a few ways that we can strengthen and accept the reality of our influential role that our Maker/husband intended for us as His royal bride.

> Influential in others' faith in Christ: Look back at the list you made of people who may be influenced by your own relationship with Christ. What ways can you be sure that they understand how you are leaning on Him during this season of sorrow in your life? List them here.

_____

_____

_____

_____

_____

_____

_____

_____

_____

Ambassador of the Gospel: We are called to bring the gospel or the good news of Christ's work on the cross to those who don't know. This is true of us in times of joy and also in times of suffering. While it may not require the exhausting task of knocking on doors or other evangelical activities while in grief, God may still bring others into your sphere of things that give you the opportunity to share the gospel with. When my Vinnie was dying in the hospital, there were many opportunities to talk to the nurses and staff about how God was working in the midst of that sad time in our lives. Many were blessed and encouraged by the stories. It even reminded and therefore encouraged me! Even in my darkest days of grief, God brought people in my life that I was able to encourage, which actually also encouraged me!

While in grief, people are more open to discussing spiritual things. If we are thankful that there's a heaven we can go to when we die and leave this earth, we should fill our hearts with joy to know we might give someone else the opportunity to believe. To be ready for such opportunities, we must pray and ask God to make us aware of those moments. We can also be ready in other ways. Check off the ways you might be better prepared for such opportunities.

___ Be ready to share your story with others, including not only the loss and sorrow but how God helped you or changed you for His glory on the journey of grief and your over all journey as a Christian.

___ Carry one or two small tracts in your purse. It's always easy to explain the gospel to someone with a listening ear when you can go through Scripture and pictures that explain what Christ did for us.

___ Carry a small Bible with you that has pages tabbed specifically where verses explain the need and work of the good news.

___ Have verses memorized to simply explain the gospel.

___ Offer to pray with someone or tell them how they can pray when they are ready to accept Christ as their Lord and Savior and become a believer in Jesus.

___ If they are a new friend, be sure to exchange contact information so you can help them find ways to begin growing in their new faith.

Be a mentor. Scripture tells us that older women are to teach the younger women (Titus 2:4). This "older" and "younger" doesn't always specifically mean age differences. It can mean a more mature Christian teaching a babe in Christ, or just helping a mature Christian through one particular area of their life where there is room for more maturity. While it might seem you don't have energy for such a task right now, if God presents the opportunity, you might find that helping someone else on her journey toward spiritual maturity might boost your healing through grief.

In many cases, mentoring comes from simply sharing your own victories with another person. Your example of trust in the Lord during your season of grief can be a natural way to mentor others. Through honestly describing your struggles and hopes with others, you give others hope that they too might experience victories in their life.

In the case of mentoring a new believer, there are wonderful little books that can help. Talk to a pastor or leader in the church, or visit your local Christian bookstore to find the right book/study.

There are no steps to becoming a mentor, because the truth is, we are always influencing others. People are watching us every day. Even our silence gives a message of who we believe we are, who our God is, and what we put our trust in. We are all mentors of others. The question to ask is: "What message does my daily action say about my God/husband and me?"

If we have not had a royalty mentality, it does take time for the reality to sink in and to become natural for us. But make no mistake, ladies, God wants us to know and experience this part of the relationship He longs to have with us. We are made to be royalty—powerful women married to the Almighty God who rules over all rulers and all things of and in the earth.

The Holy One of Israel

For your Maker is your husband—the LORD Almighty is his name—the **Holy One** of Israel is your Redeemer; he is called the God of all the earth.

Isaiah 54:5

Because I really miss Vinnie and I loved him very much, I tend to magnify the best things about him. You won't hear me talk much about the unholy Vinnie. He was hooked on old movies, and I mean hooked and obsessed. He was sometimes short-tempered. He was not always patient enough to understand the kids or me. When he was sick, he made sure I knew how miserable he was by being grumpy, whiny, and demanding at times. He, like all humans in this earthly state, was imperfect.

Please know that I am not trying to belittle or disrespect our late husbands. I am attempting, though, to honestly and gently remind us that even the best husbands aren't perfect when compared to being married to a husband who is holy.

In the biblical timeline, there was a time when husbands were perfect. Creation was the only time when humans lived exactly the way God wanted them to live—in His will and with His abundant provision. Next on the timeline was the fall of man, where the effects of sin came upon the world and began to immediately permeate all living things. Genesis 3:17-18 says, "Cursed is the ground because of you; through painful toil you will eat of it all the days of your life. It will produce thorns and thistles for you, and you will eat the plants of the field." Weeds, thistles, and a continuous labor to survive began immediately upon the disobedience of our ancestry. So did ungodly thinking and behavior.

The worldwide flood is a reflection of the anger and sorrow that God had over our fallen state. The flood wiped out almost everyone and everything, giving mankind a chance to start over. Of course God knew that even the eight people that He saved on the ark were a product of a fallen world. He knew that the sin that would follow as history unfolded would show all those of generations to come that humanity needed a more powerful way back to Him. But just to be sure, He called a particular group of people together to call His own. That group was called Israel.

In today's time, most think of Israel as a certain place, and while there was a promised land for God's people (before Christ), Israel was the name given to categorize a group of people, not a place. This group of people, the descendants of Abraham, painted the picture of the struggle between sin and holiness throughout the Bible, making it clear that religion and laws alone would never—could never—lead man directly to God.

The Israelites could never stay on track with God. The abundant "grass on the other side of the fence" continuously distracted them. They were repeatedly dissatisfied with God's plan, His timing, His provision, and His sovereignty. Does this sound like anyone you know?

Imagine for a moment that you are God in the following scene. You hear the cries of your people trapped in bondage to slavery. You give them a rescue plan out of Egypt, where they were overworked and mistreated. You help them leave the country with all their rightful possessions, including treasures and gold. You prove you are all over the plan by parting the Red Sea until the very last of your adopted people pass onto dry land. Then you just as miraculously swallow up the entire Egyptian army who has followed your trail to get you back! When all the commotion is over, you allow your people a chance to rest and wait for the second stage of this enormous rescue plan. You instruct the one you so mightily empowered to rescue the people, Moses, to come up on a mountain to receive further instruction from you. The people, waiting in the desert, get restless, and in just days, they forget their God and melt their gold, fashion it to a calf, and bow down to it (Exodus 32:2-4). As God, would you be just a bit upset with your family? You bet!

The point is this: Israel represents God's people (which now are those called believers in Jesus Christ's finished work on the cross), and the only one among the people who is holy is God Himself! Isaiah 54:5 is telling us that our heavenly husband is holy.

I think our husbands would agree with us about their own imperfections. Because of their imperfections and lack of holiness and because of our own, even the most storybook marriages were also imperfect. Because of these imperfections, we oftentimes have imperfect thinking when we lose our spouse. It is very common to experience guilt over things we did or didn't do while he was alive.

When my husband died, I thought about conversations we'd had and things I did that I later wished I could take back or change. Once he was gone, I remembered things I'd never thought of before, and I found new things to feel guilty about. I found myself wishing I could have said something else, something better, and something kinder. Can you relate to this?

For some of you, you may have neglected to forgive something that your husband said or did to you or someone in your family. It's an additional challenge in being set free from the bondage of guilt and shame when the person involved is no longer alive. It's challenging but not impossible, and until we deal with them, we can't move forward to understanding the significance of being the bride of a holy God.

Thoughts of regret or guilt are a normal part of grief. When we are in grief, we tend to only think about our own words while forgetting the context in which they were said. We tend to also neglect putting regrettable conversation in the context of the whole relationship, which was one of give and take and one of having grace. The whole journey of marriage is learning to have grace to love the other even with each other's faults. Remembering the grace given to one another throughout the marriage will oftentimes be enough to release any guilt or concern that the deceased loved one might not know how much we truly loved them. They knew it before they died, and they know it even more now.

There are times, however, that rethinking is not enough. Sometimes we must go to God and ask for His forgiveness over specifics. For instance, we can ask His forgiveness over something we might have said to our husband or repeatedly said or did. God will forgive us, and in so doing, we can be rest assured that our loved one loves us more now than they ever could while they were alive. If there are specific incidences or repeated actions that you regret or words that were spoken that need to be forgiven, please list them on the lines below. If you need to be forgiven, remember that we are not capable of forgiving ourselves. God forgives, and we can accept His forgiveness if we ask Him to forgive us.

_____

_____

_____

_____

_____

_____

_____

_____

_____

_____

_____

_____

_____

_____

_____

_____

_____

You each did things and said things in your lives together that were less than loving and kind, and yet you eventually worked out the kinks and moved forward. Why would you think it's different now? Now your loved one is wiser than he ever was while he was on earth! You may not be able to tell one another that you are sorry or forgiven, as the case may be, but we can give it to the Lord. We can assume our partner's forgiveness as we ask for the Lord's forgiveness. When you've exhausted the list, be sure to ask the Lord to forgive each thing listed, both that you forgive your husband and accept God's forgiveness for you.

What can it mean to be the wife of a holy One? You will never have to tell your heavenly husband that you forgive Him. You can trust every single decision He ever makes for you because He is just, right, and good, and He loves you more than any human being ever could. You can always trust Him; He will be the same forever, just as He was when you first met Him. He is sinless, and who He says He is, He always is. He is never changing; human beings are.

As the bride of the holy One, we can be so much more sure and confident in our role. We'll never have to work on changing Him or wishing He is more of this or too little of that. We can trust Him and worship and exalt Him. We can follow Him, place our faith and trust in His hands, and we can serve Him. What an honor to have the Holy One as our husband! It can be a worry-free life, ladies!

When we marry, most of us take on the last name of our husband. Did you know that God was given names in the Bible? If we are going to trust that God, our husband, is who He says He is, we need to search the Scriptures to find out what He tells about Himself. There are dozens and dozens of names. Let's look at a few. I've put an explanation next to some of these.

El Shaddai—Lord God Almighty (He is strong and over all things in our lives.)

El Elyon—The Most High God (There is none higher than He.)

Adonai—Lord, Master (A perfect Master over His servants)

Yahweh—Lord, Jehovah

Jehovah Nissi—The Lord My Banner (Waving the victory flag over our battle fields)

Jehovah-Raah—The Lord My Shepherd (He leads us and cares for us and attends our needs. He also speaks to His flock and those who are His sheep hear Him.)

Jehovah Rapha—The Lord That Heals (No wound or illness is too hard or too infectious for God to heal.)

Jehovah Shammah—The Lord Is There (There is nowhere we can go where the Lord will not also be!)

Jehovah Tsidkenu—The Lord Our Righteousness (We are righteous with His provision of His righteousness over us.)

Jehovah Mekoddishkem—The Lord Who Sanctifies You (He keeps working on us to make us more like Jesus every day!)

El Olam—The Everlasting God (There is no end of God.)

Qanna—Jealous (He wants our whole heart and does not want our heart to belong to another.)

Jehovah Jireh—The Lord Will Provide
(He provides everything we need. When it
seems He's not providing, we must ask if
we really need what we hope for.)

Jehovah Shalom—The Lord Is Peace
(Peace comes when there is no wrestling in
our heart and mind about God; we totally
trust Him. That is peace.)

Jehovah Sabaoth—The Lord of Hosts (He
is even Lord over all the angels.)

Jehovah El Roi—The Lord who sees
(While man creates instruments to see the
minute and that which is under the skin,
under the sea, and dazzling in the sky, God
sees it all and all at once. All things work
together because God sees it all.)

Just like the Israelites were adopted to be God's people, we too (the Gentiles) are invited to be His. The
Israelites had to sacrifice animals all the time as an
atonement or substitution for the penalty of death
they deserved for being as commonly sinful as we are
daily. Now believing in Christ's forgiveness is all we

need to enter into a holy and loving relationship with a holy God.

Some reject this, saying that it's too simplistic. It is simple but true. God is waiting to forgive the moment we go to Him, confess, ask forgiveness, and believe that Jesus was the perfect atonement, once and for all time making a way to draw us back to God, pure and simple. There's nothing we can do as humans that can make this possible for us. It doesn't take a priest to do this for us either—just a simple faith in Christ's love. You can go directly to God with this if you have accepted Christ's sacrifice (growing in a personal love relation with God by way of the cross is addressed in the introduction).

Don't get me wrong. There is a rightful place for guilt. Without it, we would never have a clue we needed to confess to God and be forgiven in the first place. But guilt doesn't have to be carried for the rest of our lives! The Holy One of Israel, the One who loves us and longs to adopt us into His family, is ready to remove the heavy backpack of guilt forever. Let Him take it and remove it. Be set free to live. He longs to make us holy as He is holy.

If a man cleanses himself from the latter, he will be an instrument for noble purposes, made holy, useful to the Master and prepared to do any good work.

2 Timothy 2:21

Both the one who makes men holy and those who are made holy are of the same family. So Jesus is not ashamed to call them brothers.

Hebrews 2:11

And by that will, we have been made holy through the sacrifice of the body of Jesus Christ once for all.

Hebrews 10:10

Because by one sacrifice he has made perfect forever those who are being made holy.

Hebrews 10:14

Our Redeemer

We are about to look at one of my personal favorite parts of this verse. Let's look at the whole verse again before we begin.

> For your Maker is your husband—the LORD Almighty is his name—the Holy One of Israel is your **Redeemer**; he is called the God of all the earth.
>
> Isaiah 54:5 (NIV)

I grew up in a violent home as a child. I was abused by my stepfather and told that I was stupid and good for nothing almost every day of my young life. I was afraid to breathe the wrong way, walk the wrong way, and to make noise or even sneeze incorrectly. I was basically afraid of everything and totally believed that every single bad thing that ever happened around me was somehow my fault. That's a terrible burden for a child to carry.

After three failed attempts at suicide as a little girl (childlike attempts like trying to staple myself until I bled to death which, as you can guess, didn't work), I began to turn to other things. For years I would live in a fantasy world with images of finding my perfect daddy someday. When it was clear that such a man didn't exist, I turned to other things that I hoped would either fill the aching hole or numb the pain of it. That resulted in four years of drug and alcohol abuse as well as many, many promiscuous relationships.

I grew up in a very dark place and carried a lot of guilt my whole life. I became a slave to my world, my heart, drugs, alcohol, and to relationships. All the things I thought I was doing to make myself better were, in the long run, only making my bondage harder to break and get out of. The pit also made me blind to seeing anything other than the ugly, dark world I was creating around me. Though, by God's grace, I was eventually rescued from that lifestyle, those years of abuse and promiscuity had a major influence on the early years of my eventual marriage to Vinnie.

Vinnie and I were not believers when we met or when we married. He found it difficult to accept that I had had many sexual relationships before him. And I did understand his dilemma. He could not grasp the fact that I was only hoping to find a love I'd longed for my whole life and didn't know where or how else to find it. He never knew such a lonely, hopeless place in his own life, so he just didn't get the logic (looking back, I can also see how illogical it really was). It became a subject that was quite taboo in our relationship. He tried to ignore his anger about it; I tried to ignore my guilt. But on more than one occasion it resurfaced unexpectedly and put an enormous wedge between us.

When I first heard Jesus referred to in Scripture as a Redeemer, I was excited to think of all the ways in which this could impact my life forever. A redeemer in biblical times was a person who would buy another person out of slavery. Picture a person who has been a slave their whole life being approached by a stranger who, without even saying hello, just whips money out of their pocket, gives it to the master, and says, "Let her go!" That is exactly what Jesus is ready to do for anyone who wants to be set free from their bondage of sin, guilt, and condemnation!

Romans 8:1 says, "There is now no condemnation for those who are in Christ Jesus." He rescues people from whatever they're in bondage to—sex, drugs, gambling, guilt, greed, gossiping, and belittling others, for example. He's waiting to rescue some widows who are in bondage to too much television, pits of depression, under or overeating, an over-obsessive solitude and withdrawal (especially from their church families), loneliness, overworking, or simply trying to ignore the pain or anger of losing their spouse. He's waiting to rescue us from whatever bondage we're in.

I've often pictured myself as a slave (to the desires of the flesh, to worry, to fear, etc.), bought miraculously by a kind and caring redeemer. I picture myself standing dumbfounded, as he might walk away. I would not know what to do next or where to go. Even though being a slave can be cruel, I imagine running after the one that just redeemed me to ask if I can serve *him* now. After all, if I only know how to serve a master, serving a man of such kindness is a wonderful alternative. Why not serve someone who's already proven they would only want good for me?

I see my relationship with God that way. I was in bondage to so many things—dark, hurtful, painful things. I accepted Jesus, He forgave me, and He redeemed me from a life with a past that was dark, and He asked if I could serve this good master. He does desire us to serve Him. We were made to serve Him. But in my case, I didn't surrender all my baggage. I tried to serve Him and carried the heavy backpack of my past along with me. Carrying this unnecessary load affected my marriage and other relationships.

On one of those rare occasions when something of my ugly past resurfaced in a conversation, the wedge between Vinnie and me also returned. Though we were believers at this point, Vinnie didn't like me and wouldn't talk to me for days. It was just the pattern we'd had when this subject arose at other times in our past. Please understand that it's not that he *really* didn't like me anymore. He just didn't like who he saw me to be when he was reminded that I had not always been a good little girl. He was a very good man, but in his eyes, at that moment, I was not a very good woman. He simply didn't know what to do with that.

On this particular occasion, unlike my pre-Christ days, I spent three days in prayer. I even fasted and begged God to show me what I was to do in this situation. Vinnie would barely acknowledge I was in the room. We simply went through the motions of being friends, but the air between us was as cold as ice.

On the third day, God's love hit me like a ton of bricks. The blood that Jesus shed on the cross was for the purpose of washing that sinful past of mine away—for good! Psalm 103:12 says, "As far as the east is from the west, so far has he removed our transgressions from us." Jesus did this for me so I would have a pure and holy, deep, and intimate relationship with Him! It hit me; I was no longer that ugly woman from the past. I'd been redeemed!

I went to Vinnie in a soft voice that had no undertones of guilt. I simply said something like, "I can't make you like me again. I can't make you forgive me. I can't change the way you see me, but I can tell you that the person you don't like right now doesn't even exist anymore. She was washed away by the sacrifice Jesus made on the cross, and she was bought out at a high cost. She was redeemed. She is dead." I was absolutely, positively sure of how God saw me at that moment—a pure and holy bride of Christ. What a miraculous realization of the transformation God had already done! I told Vinnie that I would pray that

God would give him God's eyes so he could see me the way God did: beautiful, radiant, and lovely.

God must have answered that prayer, because the subject never came up again, not because we did a better job of ignoring guilt and anger, but because God literally took the issue right out of our lives. We actually loved each other more from that day forward than ever before in our relationship.

I have been a slave to my circumstances, feelings, lies, the world, and all kinds of things. My master at one time was drugs, alcohol, cigarettes, immorality, and all the things of the world. I was under the influence of a master who told me how to fix that hole in my heart. And even though that master led me to only feel a bigger hole in my heart, I didn't know how to be anything but a slave to this ugly master. The hole got bigger as I got older, and my world got darker and darker. It all became a vicious cycle. I was under its command on my life, and I was a slave to it.

Maybe you have a past. It might be as ugly as mine was. Maybe yours is a secret little something you feel guilt over. Maybe it's one single word or action you experienced while you were married. Maybe it's a lifetime of trouble. No matter what, Jesus wants to wipe it clean. He wants to redeem you even of guilt and shame. He wants to redeem you from the world you have been master of, even if you created that ugly world all by yourself.

Remember, Romans 8:1 says, "Therefore, there is now no condemnation for those who are in Christ Jesus." Do you see that little two-letter word in there? It's "no" condemnation. Mind you, there's plenty of condemnation before the redemption, but if you allow Jesus to forgive you, He will also redeem you from the hold of its guilt as well. He will redeem you to a new life, even if the guilt is over something that was said or done to your husband who is no longer here to personally forgive you himself. That is one of the most freeing realities of all times.

Are there any areas of your past that you experience guilt for? Is there a dark world you still dwell in at times or all the time? Write down circumstances that come to mind. God knows all those secret things and places too, so be honest and be thorough. It doesn't matter how big or small or often or infrequent these things occurred; if it comes to mind, write it down.

_____

_____

_____

_____

_____

_____

_____

_____

_____

_____

_____

_____

_____

_____

_____

Remember, you can keep coming back to this as things come to mind, even months later. Jesus can redeem us from all the masters we've served. Even though it's painful, each area of our past must be stared at right in the face, and Jesus will come along and remind us that we've been bought right out of its bondage. God wants to forgive you and take you right out of the master of a world of sin to one of His goodness and love.

God of All the Earth

> For your Maker is your husband—the
> LORD Almighty is his name—the Holy
> One of Israel is your Redeemer; he is called
> the **God of all the earth**.
>
> Isaiah 54:5 (NIV)

Our husband's domain encompassed his family, home,
work, and community. This is how God designed it
for mankind as we read in Genesis, the book of God's
creation story.

> And God said, "Let the land produce living
> creatures according to their kinds: livestock,
> creatures that move along the ground, and
> wild animals, each according to its kind."
> And it was so. God made the wild ani-
> mals according to their kinds, the livestock

according to their kinds, and all the creatures that move along the ground according to their kinds. And God saw that it was good. Then God said, "Let us make man in our image, in our likeness, and let them rule over the fish of the sea and the birds of the air, over the livestock, over all the earth, and over all the creatures that move along the ground." So God created man in his own image, in the image of God he created him; male and female he created them. God blessed them and said to them, "Be fruitful and increase in number; fill the earth and subdue it. Rule over the fish of the sea and the birds of the air and over every living creature that moves on the ground."

Genesis 1:24-28

God is God over all creation, including you and your life. He knows all things. He's sovereign over all things. He has a solution to all problems. He even has a plan for your life as a widow! Death was not God's plan for us, but it is part of this fallen state we are in. This is a temporary state, because the Bible does say that a time will come when all sorrow and death will end. Revelation 21:4 says, "He will wipe every tear from their eyes. There will be no more death or mourning or crying or pain, for the old order of things has passed away." As Paul Tripp puts it, "Death will be put to death!"

But until that time comes, death will invade everyone's life, and if you are reading this book, it's come to your own life too. It's necessary to be reminded of this, because though God does not like death any more than we do, even though He does not want death, He is God over your life and your life without your husband. Though God did not want us to experience death, while we still live in this era of fallen state, the days of each person are numbered according to God's Sovereign plan (Job 14:5). He knows you have a huge gap in your heart and life now that your husband is gone. He knows your needs. He knows the plans for your future too! "'For I know the plans I have for you,'" declares the LORD, "'plans to prosper you and not to harm you, plans to give you hope and a future'" (Jeremiah 29:11). He was God over your life before you were a widow, and He is God over your life now.

I mentioned earlier that I'd started a new job just a few weeks before Vinnie's diagnosis with cancer. It was difficult to stay focused at times, especially when the cancer progressed and we made so many trips to the emergency room. My employer tried to be patient and understanding, but the many distracting phone calls, and of course the sudden need to get up and rush home, became more than my concentration could handle. When Vinnie died, and then Michael (and a good friend of mine died the same day from a sudden heart attack), I was still unable to have good focus on my work. I loved my job, but the lack of ability to do my job well became more frustrating every day for both my employer and me.

Because of budget cuts, there was a need to eliminate someone from the payroll. It was a no-brainer when I became the chosen candidate. Even a year after Vinnie's death, my work was not improving, and looking back, I can see that my attitude was not always Christ-like. I was asked to leave. The job that I praised God for providing for me a year before Vinnie's death was now slipped out from under me a year after Vinnie's death. My first reaction was to panic, especially when I learned that I would not qualify for unemployment because I'd been working for a nonprofit where they had opted out of having to pay unemployment insurance.

As I drove home on the day of this terrifying news, weeping chaotically while crying out to God, "What am I do to now?" in a tiny moment of silence (perhaps to catch a breath), I suddenly felt a sense of relief that at least I'd get to experience some rest I knew had been lacking in my life for two years. Though I learned in GriefShare that sleeplessness is a common effect of grief, I never heard of any remedies to offset it. Not working for a while presented tremendous challenges financially, especially without receiving unemployment, and I was too young to receive Social Security benefits, but I suddenly felt peace. It seemed like God was saying to me, "You've had two restless years pushing yourself beyond your own ability to cope with everything on your plate. It's now time for you to rest. Take advantage of this time. Rest and don't feel guilty about it. I'm providing this time for you to rest, and I'll take care of the rest."

I have to confess that I was not initially obedient to the call to rest. I immediately started looking for a job. It was beyond my ability to grasp that I wouldn't work at least part time. I didn't want to appear lazy to anyone or irresponsible if I might have to ask for some help financially. I immediately took a job working at a counseling agency. I loved the environment and the people, but it didn't take long for both my employer, coworkers, and myself to see that I had no more ability to do a good job working for them than I did in my previous employment. I resigned within two months. At this point, the Lord made it clear that I was to stay unemployed for a while so I could rest. In fact, it seemed like the Lord was suggesting (somewhere deep down in those ears made for God's place in my soul), "You've got until June. Rest until then. I'll take care of you."

None of this was part of the plan I thought was to take place after Vinnie's death. I envisioned working full time and resuming my old regimen of church activities and family visits. I was not sure where the funds were to come from week to week, but I tried to live frugally on the life insurance money I had left at that point, and God provided some astonishing gifts of financial support and even physical help in my home during those six months of rest. And to top it off, I actually responded to a job posting on May 31 (the only one I sent a résumé to), was interviewed and hired the same day (after being told initially that the owner had pretty much decided already who he was going to hire). I started my new full-time job on June 2.

If you question that God's not doing a good job at taking care of some part of your life, maybe you should be asking if He has a better plan than yours. He *is* God of all the earth, even your earth. Sometimes we get frustrated because we see a need, we pray, and it seems like God's not answering or He's saying no. Sometimes He is saying, "Wait," but sometimes He *is* saying no because He has a different plan. Wrestle with God over these things. He has a plan, and we must discern His plan and be willing to move forward with it, trusting His love and wisdom in planning our lives! You can believe God's love for you, and when you do, you will know that He's not out to get you or punishing you for something. God disciplines, yes, but that means He's trying to teach us something because He loves us. Trust that and then look around to see what He might be doing around you. Circumstances cannot be the factor that determines whether God's turned away from us or if He exists.

He is oftentimes asking us to change something in our life. For instance, you might be struggling financially. You might live in a large home and can't take care of it on your own, but you don't want to leave. Perhaps you ask God to provide a job so you don't have to move. However, God might know (better than we do at the time) our lives would be simpler if we moved to an apartment, a smaller home, or even a townhome where someone else would take care of the grounds. Perhaps he has a plan for you to find someone to rent a room to for income, or for company to fill the evenings now filled with too much silence. Perhaps it's even someone He wants you to minister to. He could be asking you to move, knowing that where He'll take you will bring you greater blessing than staying put.

Of course, I can't answer these types of questions for you, and you don't want to make any big decisions too soon after your spouse has died. You have to wrestle this out with God Himself, between Him and you, and perhaps also the advice of many wise and objective friends who care about your well being. But make no bones about it, God is ever changing us and wanting to change us to become more like Jesus. He knows we'll find our joy in *that*, and it oftentimes requires changes in our worlds. Besides, your world's already changed, drastically. Holding on to the life and lifestyle you had while your spouse was alive is futile. It will never be the same, and trying to keep it the same will only slow down your ability to heal, discern God's new plan for you, and adjust.

Don't be afraid of change! When it comes from God, it's only going to bring you greater blessing and make you eventually more like Jesus where your joy will be made complete. Be still enough to listen and open minded enough to seek the possibility of a new plan, one that has nothing to do with the agenda that might have been on your mind to start with.

Sometimes we have to take Proverbs 3 to heart: "Trust in the LORD with all your heart and lean not on your own understanding; in all your ways acknowledge him, and he will make your paths straight" (Proverbs 3:5-6). God's ways don't always make sense to us, at least initially, but He is God over all creation, your entire world! By not answering a prayer our way, it's sometimes His way of helping us think of another way to do something, another place to live, another job to take, or another role to play. We must get to a place where we no longer question why God doesn't do things we expect or wish or in the ways we hope or desire. We need to instead ask Him if we are going about lives our own way and if He is trying to show us a different path.

Let's take a moment right now to pray. We're going to ask God to show us areas of our lives that He's asking us to change. Let's ask God to show us if there are new paths that lie ahead of us and new horizons in our future. Let's ask God to open our minds and hearts to see and hear what He might be telling us so our lives can line up with His sovereign plan for our lives—a plan that fits in the puzzle of His greater plan of restoring His kingdom on earth.

> Dear heavenly Father, I know that there are still so many layers to be revealed and removed. Like the silversmith that melts and stirs the silver and skims the dross off the top over and over again until he sees his perfect reflection in the melted metal, you are making me more and more like your Son every day. Show me things in my life and heart that need to be peeled away. Show me thinking that I've carried around for years and years that have no part with your Truth, and remove it! Show me the areas of my life that need to be nailed to the cross, put to death, and never taken back

again. Show me how to be the woman you created me to be and to do the things you desire for me to do. If that requires that I move or change my job, or make any other major changes in my life or lifestyle, give me discernment to sense it, the confidence to trust that, and the courage and excitement to carry out your plan. If I'm uncomfortable with change, show me how to rely on your ability to strengthen and equip me. Lord, give me whatever it takes to follow you and to make my life about *you*, not *me*. Take away my fears and anxieties and even my rebellion. Show me the new direction you have for my life now that I'm no longer married, and give me joy again, including a joy in being your child and your bride. I pray this all in Jesus's name. Amen.

You may find yourself needing to pray this prayer many, many times and for many months. As thoughts come to you while you pray, write them down. This may help you solidify areas of your life that the Lord is trying to teach you, reveal to you, or change. Use the space below for the following exercise:

_____ _____

_____ _____

_____ _____

_____ _____

_____ _____

_____ _____

_____ _____

_____ _____

_____ _____

_____ _____

_____ _____

_____ _____

_____ _____

_____ _____

Make a list in the left column of areas that you need God's help with in your world. This might be for a job or a new job, making a decision to sell your home or move to another location, to invest in a new retirement plan, to find help in fixing the roof, mowing the lawn, or looking for trustworthy maintenance on your car. As you learn to trust that He is God of all the earth, including little pieces of it, begin praying for and about these things with the expectancy that God will answer, and to be open to hear the answer that God has for you. Take notes each day of how you sense God is answering these prayers and write these as they come to you in the column on the right, near the prayer request on the left (although you may eventually need a whole new page for this exercise. I use entire notebooks!).

It is my prayer that this exercise will be an eye-opening experience for you. It is an excellent tool in developing the vision needed for seeing God's fingerprints at work in your life and all around you. Go back and read the passage from Genesis written at the beginning of this section (Genesis 1:24-2). Do you see what a busy God we have? He created the earth and all the life in it and is still busy looking after all of it. He even empowered us to partner with Him in taking care of the earth, giving each of us our small section to be good stewards over. We need exercises like this to discern His plan, because His plan is the only one that is going to last, will have significance in His big scheme of things, and bring us the greatest joy and fulfillment while we're still here on earth!

Conclusion

If you have read and even begun to do some of the exercises in this book, I hope you are beginning to feel yourself changing and/or beginning to see a glimmer of light at the end of what might have once seemed a long, endless tunnel ahead. And I pray that your understanding of God—who He says He is and who you are in Christ—is all beginning to change in your mind and heart. Though we are forgiven of our sins when we accept Christ as our Lord and Savior, He is also in the continuous process of making us more like Jesus every day. He is continuously reshaping us.

> Yet, O LORD, you are our Father. We are the clay, you are the potter; we are all the work of your hand.
>
> Isaiah 64:8

God gives us a beautiful picture of this transformation in the example of the butterfly's transformation. I think it best illustrates the journey of the widow. After all, Romans 1:20 tells us, "For since the creation of the world God's invisible qualities—his eternal power and divine nature—have been clearly seen, being understood from what has been made, so that men are without excuse." In order for God to use you, you must move with Him like waves of the ocean. We belong to Him. If you allow God to use you, you will begin to also see how it is that God will reveal the new life He has for you now.

Let's look at the metaphor of a caterpillar as it relates to being a widow. It's important to understand the stages that are normal for us to go through as widows. There is a time in grief where we crawl into a cocoon and hide. It's a natural place to go and a place we should go to for a while, but it's important to not get stuck there.

While in the cocoon, it might seem dark, and you may lose sight of the Son. Paul Tripp paints a picture for us in the GriefShare ministry video series. He has the participants think about being in a basement with covers over the windows. One standing in the dark basement might wonder if the sun has vanished because they see no light at all. But when someone begins to pull back the curtains, it becomes clear that the sun was there all the while. Not seeing the sun doesn't mean it doesn't exist any more, just as not experiencing God means He doesn't exist.

While in the cocoon, it appears to someone looking in that nothing is happening. But the real work is going on inside (if we allow God to work by knowing that He's still with us). We don't have to see the work. We have to believe He's at work. Just believe His Word is true. In time, the cocoon begins to crack. More of the sun (or in this case, Son) is seen and experienced. Little by little, the old peels away and a completely new creation (and life) emerges: a butterfly.

Interestingly enough, the escape from the cocoon is a long, difficult struggle. I recently heard a story of a little boy who had a butterfly nest. After waiting and watching the process of the caterpillar becoming a cocoon and then seeing the early stages of the butterfly's emergence into the world, the little boy became concerned about the butterfly's fight to get out. He ran to get scissors and carefully snipped part of the cocoon away, instantly releasing the butterfly from its snag. Sadly, the butterfly fell to the bottom of the net and flapped around a few hours, eventually withering up to die. The boy later learned that the struggle to escape is part of the process of readying the butterfly for the ability to fly. Without the struggle, the butterfly wings don't get the air necessary to fully dry so the butterfly can exit from the cocoon and live. The wings of the little boy's butterfly were too heavy with moisture to take flight, an act of seeming kindness, an attempt to rescue that cost the butterfly's life. Take note: there are no shortcuts to God's plan when He is developing things He has stored up for our lives. As painful as some parts of the journey are, remaining at peace with God, trusting His Sovereign plan for our lives and His love for us, we can begin to eventually experience the blessing of becoming the beautiful woman God intends.

In the process of God's plan, there's nothing of the butterfly that resembles the caterpillar it once was. The colors aren't the same. It sprouts wings it never had before. It grows antennae in the cocoon that it never had before, and it soars in the air, seeing the world from a whole new perspective—from above it. That's quite a different view of the world after seeing the world from the perspective of crawling on the ground.

God's desire is always for us to know Him and to become more like Him. When we become more like

Him, we will love others like He commands us to. We will love Him like He deserves, and we will shine like Him in this dark world. God uses all things to the good of those who love Him—even the death of your spouse. He has things He wants to show you so you will become more like Jesus.

If you cannot imagine knowing joy again, that is fine for now. You are still in the early part of your grief. It's a sad, sad place. But know this: if you want to be healed, look that pain in the face. Do things that bring tears, if you have tears that you fight back all day. You are not *creating* tears by doing this. You are *releasing* tears already in you that are waiting to come out. Tears cleanse and are a part of what God gave us to be healed. To use the analogy of the butterfly, if you try to fly without releasing all the moisture encased in the cocoon, you won't be able to soar like God intends if you rush to get out of that struggling experience.

If we use the analogy of a wounded heart, we can easily see that wounds that aren't tended to get infected. And it's oftentimes very painful to tend the wound but quite necessary. Healing from grief is the same. We must face the pain. But let this be known that you have permission to live again! You have permission to have joy again! You can love again! You not only *can*, but you *must*. You gain nothing, not even honor from your lost loved one, by holding onto false loyalty and trying to keep hold of the past. Our husbands know life now like they never knew it while they were here on earth. And so must we. That would honor them! Let me put it another way, a way the Lord made clear to me one day while sitting a traffic light.

As a soldier drove by, I asked the Lord if I'd be missing Vinnie the same if he weren't dead but was instead deployed and I were home waiting for his return. I heard these words in my heart almost immediately: "Gail, you don't have the picture right. Vinnie is home. You are still deployed. Fight the good fight until it's time for you to come home. Your work here is not finished."

Ladies, there is work for us to be done here. What's the good fight? It's to regain joy each morning, fighting against the temptation to complain and not go on. It's the fight for souls who are aching and crying out for help and helping them find the One and only who can help and heal them. It's the fight fought on our knees to bring restoration to our families and relationships, and it's a fight to love those around us like they too might not be here tomorrow. It's standing firm in the knowledge that

God is our Maker, our husband, the Almighty One of all His people. It's standing firm in the knowledge that you were redeemed for such a time as this, for strangers, for your family, for the church. It's standing firm on the solid ground, even while you're feeling you're crumbling inside, clinging to the truth that you are a beautiful bride to Him, and, like royalty, you shine with value.

Grieve while it's time to grieve, but march on, dear one. Beg God to help you understand so when the time comes, you are ready to allow God to fill you with the knowledge of these things in your life and you will shine like a light on a hill for His glory!

The relationship between a husband and wife is intimate. God wants an intimate relationship with each of us too—yes, with you! In the Garden of Eden, God walked among Adam and Eve. Imagine seeing God with our own eyes walking right next to us. It's a breathtaking idea! Because we live in a fallen world, He cannot walk with us like that (yet), but through the person of Jesus, we can experience God as our husband in very intimate ways and at times when we really need Him (like when we come home to an empty house). We grow in this intimacy through a life of prayer and being attentive to the ways He speaks to us throughout the day and in His Word. I've been so desperate for God at times that I could literally feel His arms around me.

I hope you can hear what I am saying; God wants you to know Him as your husband! He wants you to know Him as the best husband you could ever dream of! He wants to protect and rescue you like no one ever could. He wants to forgive you for your faults more than any man can or will ever see the need for. He wants you to know you are precious, purposeful, and even vital to carrying out His big plan of action— a new heaven and a new earth. We each play a part in this battle against evil/sin and God/goodness.

Let God be your husband now and forever, even if you remarry someday. Know Him as husband while you no longer have an earthly husband. If you remarry, your renewed intimacy with God will build an even sweeter relationship with the new spouse. When I married Mike almost three years after Vinnie's death, I knew it would be different than the marriage I had with Vinnie, not because I loved one more than the other, but because I had become a different person in my season of grief and healing. I'd learned to find a joy in the Lord that no man or death of one could ever erase from my life. But whether you remarry or not, all will be sweeter when your relationship with God is what it could be. Your whole life will be sweeter because of the powerful relationship God desires to have with you. Release your worries, guilt, and your life to the One who is God over all things on earth, including you.

We all need help at times dusting off the antennas to know where He is and how He wants to satisfy completely! Reading the Bible, daily prayer, and taking continued inventory of what we sense God's doing in our lives will do the dusting. Join me on the journey of discovering who our husband *really* is. Let's challenge each other and the women in our sphere of influence to know to whom it is we are married! Heal when it's time to heal, and while we do, let's live the lives as the beautiful women we were meant to be. Let's live up to the highest calling known to man: to be the bride of a holy God, the Lord God Almighty, our Maker, and let us allow Him to show us how He longs to be the perfect husband to each of us.

Additional meditation: In this book, we've seen God referred to as our Maker, our husband, Lord of lords, a holy God, and Redeemer. God is each of these things and more. They are inseparable descriptions of who God is and who we are to Him. He is God. I've added some additional Scriptures here for you reflect on. Put them on your bathroom mirror, your dashboard, desk, or refrigerator door and make a mental note each day as to whether you are experiencing yourself and God in the ways He desires and has described in these verses. Read them (and Isaiah 54:5) again and again, making personal notes and writing down the prayer of your heart to experience the relationships described in each. It is God's desire for you to experience Him in the ways described in each of these passages.

The bride belongs to the bridegroom.

John 3:29

I delight greatly in the LORD; my soul rejoices in my God. For he has clothed me with garments of salvation and arrayed me in a robe of righteousness, as a bridegroom adorns his head like a priest, and as a bride adorns herself with her jewels.

Isaiah 61:10

Let us rejoice and be glad and give him glory! For the wedding of the Lamb has come, and his bride has made herself ready.

Revelation 19:7

I saw the Holy City, the new Jerusalem, coming down out of heaven from God, prepared as a bride beautifully dressed for her husband.

Revelation 21:2

One of the seven angels who had the seven bowls full of the seven last plagues came and said to me, "Come, I will show you the bride, the wife of the Lamb.

Revelation 21:9

The Spirit and the bride say, "Come!" And let him who hears say, "Come!" Whoever is thirsty, let him come; and whoever wishes, let him take the free gift of the water of life.

Revelation 22:17